W9-CFQ-302

The

SOUTHERN EDUCATION

of a

JERSEY GIRL

*Adventures in Life and Love
in the Heart of Dixie*

Jaime Primak Sullivan

with Eve Adamson

TOUCHSTONE

New York   London   Toronto   Sydney   New Delhi

Touchstone
An Imprint of Simon & Schuster, Inc.
1230 Avenue of the Americas
New York, NY 10020

First Touchstone hardcover edition August 2016

TOUCHSTONE and colophon are registered trademarks of Simon & Schuster, Inc.

For information about special discounts for bulk purchases, please contact Simon & Schuster Special Sales at 1-866-506-1949 or business@simonandschuster.com.

The Simon & Schuster Speakers Bureau can bring authors to your live event. For more information or to book an event, contact the Simon & Schuster Speakers Bureau at 866-248-3049 or visit our website at www.simonspeakers.com.

Interior design by Jill Putorti
Lip art © Shutterstock

Manufactured in the United States of America

10 9 8 7 6 5 4 3

Library of Congress Cataloging-in-Publication Data

Names: Sullivan, Jaime Primak, author. | Adamson, Eve, co-author.
Title: The Southern education of a Jersey girl : adventures in life and love in the heart of Dixie / Jaime Primak Sullivan with Eve Adamson.
Description: New York : Touchstone, 2016.
Identifiers: LCCN 2015050489 (print) | LCCN 2016016389 (ebook) | ISBN 9781501115370 (hardback) | ISBN 9781501115479 (ebook)
Subjects: LCSH: Sullivan, Jaime Primak. | Sullivan, Jaime Primak—Marriage. | Young women—Alabama—Birmingham—Biography. | Birmingham (Ala.)—Social life and customs. | Women—Southern States—Social life and customs. | Southern States—Social life and customs. | Birmingham (Ala.)—Biography. | New Jersey—Biography. | Television personalities—United States—Biography. | Public relations—United States—Biography. | BISAC: BIOGRAPHY & AUTOBIOGRAPHY / Personal Memoirs. | FAMILY & RELATIONSHIPS / Love & Romance. | PERFORMING ARTS / Television / General.
Classification: LCC F334.B653 S85 2016 (print) | LCC F334.B653 (ebook) | DDC 791.45092 [B] —dc23
LC record available at https://lccn.loc.gov/2015050489

ISBN 978-1-5011-1537-0
ISBN 978-1-5011-1547-9 (ebook)

For real women everywhere.

[Yankees] are pretty much like southerners except
with worse manners, of course, and terrible accents.

—MARGARET MITCHELL,
GONE WITH THE WIND

Manners involve the appearance of things,
rather than the total reality.

—*MISS MANNERS' GUIDE TO
EXCRUCIATINGLY CORRECT BEHAVIOR*

Everyone in the South has no time for
reading because they are all too busy writing.

—WILLIAM FAULKNER

Note: In this book, I make some assumptions and generalizations about both the North and the South. I do this with the full realization that generalizations are not always true. The North isn't all like Jersey—*my* Jersey isn't even all like Jersey. Just as the South isn't all like Alabama, and *my* Alabama isn't like all of Alabama. This book is about my experience, and contains my personal observations. I hope no one will take offense. None is intended.

CONTENTS

Introduction
LOVING THE LIFE THAT IS   xiii

Part One
GOD BLESS THE BROKEN ROAD   1

Chapter 1: THE POWER OF A GREAT PAIR OF JEANS   3

Chapter 2: BREAKING UP IS EASY   17

Chapter 3: THE KISS EXPERIMENT   25

Chapter 4: "HONEY, HE'S GAY"   31

Chapter 5: DADDY ISSUES   43

Chapter 6: AND THEN HE KISSED ME   55

Chapter 7: TAMPONS, HUMILIATION, AND THE ULTIMATE PRIZE   61

Chapter 8: ROSE-COLORED GLASSES   71

Chapter 9: LA WOMAN   91

Chapter 10: YANKEE IMPATIENCE AND THE QUEST FOR THE RING   103

Chapter 11: THE GREATEST LOVE STORY EVER TOLD   109

Chapter 12: "SURELY NOT"   121

Chapter 13: "THESE ARE NOT MY PEOPLE"   131

Part Two
THE LONGEST YEAR   137

Chapter 14: PLEASANTVILLE   139

Chapter 15: BRITNEY SPEARS AND THE SWEET TEA EXPERIMENT   149

Chapter 16: THREE PARTIES AND A WEDDING   157

CONTENTS

Chapter 17: SNOT ROCKETS FIRED IN THE GOVERNOR'S MANSION   165

Chapter 18: SECRETS, LIES, AND LUCK   181

Chapter 19: AGAINST ALL ODDS   185

Chapter 20: I'M MARRYING BOTH OF YOU   191

Part Three
SOUTHERN METAMORPHOSIS   201

Chapter 21: IT'S A BOY! OR IS IT?   203

Chapter 22: SCARLETT—MY EMERGENCY CONTACT   211

Chapter 23: BABY BELLE   215

Chapter 24: BABY LOVE AND LOSS   221

Chapter 25: ADRIENNE: BECAUSE EVERY BRUNETTE NEEDS A BLONDE   229

Chapter 26: CHARLIE   247

Chapter 27: DANIELLE, MY BELLE   249

Chapter 28: SAVED BY THE BELLES   253

Chapter 29: WHERE ARE THEY NOW?   263

Chapter 30: REAL WOMEN ARE A WORK IN PROGRESS   269

ACKNOWLEDGMENTS   275

LOVING THE LIFE THAT IS

"*I* hear Thursday's going to be bad in New York," my assistant told me. "I hope you can make your flight."

"What, it might snow?" I said, rolling my eyes. "I'm not afraid of a little snow."

Living in Alabama, I encounter a lot of snow-ignorance. People in the South think snow is some kind of natural disaster. The mere mention of the word and everybody panics. Should we actually see a flurry? Cars slide off the roads. School gets canceled. Don't waste your time at the Piggly Wiggly; you can all but forget about bread and milk. I'm from Jersey, so I think this is a little ridiculous. Snow is no big deal. When you grow up with it, you learn how to love it.

But all that week, people kept mentioning it, or pulling up the weather maps on their phones. "Ugh, look at this weather moving in. There's no way you're going to get into New York on Thursday."

"Oh, come on," I said, over and over. "I've seen this a million times. It's nothing. A week out, they say eight inches of snow, and then it's five, and then it's three inches, and then you barely get a dusting. Besides, it's New York. I think they know how to handle a little cold weather," I concluded, implying to my over-reactive southern friends that they, by contrast, did not.

But the day before I was scheduled to leave, I got an email that my flight was canceled. Come on, are you kidding me? I called Delta and I waited forty-seven minutes on hold. When I finally got a human being, I was Yankee-insistent. I had no time for manners.

"My flight was canceled and I need to get to New York. I have two scheduled appearances. I do not have the option of a no-show."

"The weather in New York is supposed to be really bad," the sympathetic Delta rep said with a warm southern accent. "Right now, we only have two flights still scheduled to go out of Atlanta." So much for my convenient nonstop flight, but Birmingham to Atlanta to New York was better than missing the Jersey Cawfeetawk event five months in the making. I heard the tapping of computer keys. "It looks like we've already rebooked you on the later of the last two flights going out," he said.

"No. Put me on the earlier one. If the weather's really supposed to be as bad as they say, that later flight's not getting out."

"I can keep you in first class. You'll be in the first seat on the left-hand side of the plane," he said.

"Perfect."

Little did I know that seat would turn out to be the scariest seat in the house.

That morning, having already endured a cancellation, a rebooking, and a re-rebooking, I was on my way to the airport at five thirty AM when I got a call from the kids' school: closed in anticipation of the approaching inclement weather. I never leave town when they close school, but I was hell-bound for New York and I couldn't change my plans now. I called my husband, Michael.

"Babe, school's canceled."

"All right. I won't go to Montgomery. I'll stay in Birmingham." My husband is a lobbyist, and he just happened to have a flexible schedule that day.

At the airport at last, I breathed a sigh of relief. Home and family secured, I was back to work. Only I wasn't. As I approached the security line, I realized I'd forgotten my driver's license. In all my years of flying, I've never forgotten my license. I was beginning to think something was trying to keep me in Alabama. I went through some rigorous security checks, but because they seemed to know me from TV or because I travel so often, they let me through.

When I got to the gate, I asked the gate agent, "Is my connection in Atlanta still on time?"

"As of now it is, but the weather in New York doesn't look good."

"So I've heard," I mumbled.

The flight to Atlanta was uneventful. I hadn't sat to shoot my Cawfeetawk video for the day yet, so I recorded it in the Atlanta airport. Every morning, I sit down with my cup of coffee and my iPhone and talk about something that's been on my mind. I decided to share my thoughts on how to say a proper good-bye to someone who's dying. I talked about my experience with my dad, and what I wish I had done differently when he died.

At the gate, there was a lot of buzz about whether the flight to LaGuardia would be canceled or not, but it remained on time. Still on time. Still on time. They boarded us and suddenly, after all my dismissal of the situation, something about the flight made me uneasy. Before we took off, I went up to the flight attendants.

"I want you guys to have a safe flight." I gave them both hugs. When the captain stepped out of the cockpit to say something to the flight attendants, he heard me.

"We're going to be just fine," he said. "We're going to be great. Icy rain scares me, but snow? Snow doesn't scare me."

"It scares me," I said. After all my efforts to get here, I was second-guessing my cavalier attitude.

"Well, we're going to be fine," he said. "Don't worry."

Everything seemed to be going smoothly as we approached LaGuardia, but the clouds were very thick. There was no visibility. I heard the flight attendants whispering about how the pilot had asked for a holding pattern but hadn't been granted one. His voice filled the cabin: "Well, folks, we thought we would be put in a stay, but it looks like they're bringing us in, so flight attendants, prepare the cabin for landing and expect it to be bumpy."

As we came through the clouds, the distance to the runway was surprisingly short. We were almost on top of it and it was covered in snow. There was nobody next to me, so I looked across the aisle at the man sitting there. "We're not going to make it," I whispered.

Then we hit the runway and the pilot engaged the brakes . . . and nothing happened. There was no slowing down. The brakes didn't take. The wheels couldn't find anything to grip. You know how when you land, there's that rush of the engines in reverse thrust that pushes you forward into your seat? There was none of that. We were skidding and sliding and in seconds, I could tell we were off the runway, the plane bumping and jolting and still careening through the snow with no sign of slowing down. We were on the ground, but what would stop us? Then I saw the water. It was coming right at us.

Inside the plane, there was a controlled panic, people wide-eyed, gripping their armrests, some of them stricken and silent with fear, some crying out. We careened toward the water, nothing between us and the bay but a flimsy-looking safety fence that I knew wouldn't stop us. I could see that it couldn't stop us. My brain was going as fast as the plane: *Do planes sink or float? If we hit the water, will the windows break? Will we drown in the icy bay? How fast can rescue get to us? Will I ever see my kids again? Do I need to call Michael and tell him—what? This is the end?* My life literally flashed before my eyes—I saw it all, how every decision I had ever made led me to that plane.

Then the left side of the plane hit a fence and we lost our left wing. The power went out. We continued to slide. The plane slammed into a berm of earth built up between the runway and Flushing Bay. It was the most powerfully jarring and abrupt physical sensation I'd ever felt. The nose of the plane rode up the berm, smashed through the fence at the top, and came to a stop, hanging over the water. I looked out my window. The water, not yet frozen, lapped the snowy shore beneath me. If I could have opened the window and jumped out, I would have landed in it. If it hadn't been for that raised berm, we would be in a very different situation.

There was a moment of shocked silence, except for the

woman behind me, who was sobbing hysterically. I grabbed my phone and, without really thinking about it, just wanting to share my experience with the people I cared about, I tweeted:

We just crash landed at LGA. I'm terrified. Please pray . . .

I looked around me. Was it over? Was the plane about to explode? Were we safe, or still in peril? The flight attendant got on a handheld bullhorn. "Is everyone okay? We have no power, and the emergency slides didn't inflate, so we are all going to have to exit off the wing of the plane." The left wing was smashed. That left a damaged right wing—our only possible exit.

The pilot stumbled out of the cockpit. We locked eyes and I could see he was terrified. I burst into tears. I couldn't hold it in anymore. I imagined him seeing that water coming at us a hundred miles an hour. He must have been thinking, *I have to save these people.* He came over to me and put a hand on my shoulder. "You're okay," he said. "I'm going to get you off this plane."

I was the last passenger off. As everyone filed toward the door and climbed out onto the wing, it was like a movie—there was fire, ice, snow falling, snow all over the ground, people crying. Twenty-eight people were injured in the crash. Five were taken to the hospital. Everyone survived.

Once we were all off the plane, they put us on a shuttle to take us back to the terminal. As the shuttle took off, my phone rang. It was CNN, wanting to know what happened.

"What? How did you know?" I mumbled.

"I saw your tweet."

I don't even remember how I answered. When I hung up, I sent another tweet:

We have all been evacuated. Everyone is safe. Thank you for your prayers. God is good.

As we all filed into the terminal, I looked around me. It was surreal. Life was going on all around us, despite our trauma. There we were, 127 people in shock, walking through an airport filled with people drinking in bars, eating at restaurants, talking on their phones, hammering away at their laptops. People acting much like I had been acting just hours before. They had no idea what had just happened to us. I wanted to stop and scream, *Don't you realize that life can change in a minute?* Of course, I couldn't do that. But I felt like my life *had* changed. For all these people, on their way to somewhere else, it was still business as usual.

We were taken to a Delta Sky Lounge for processing. They brought us water and snacks as the EMTs checked everybody out. We had to answer questions, deal with luggage, calm down. After three hours, those of us who didn't need medical care were deemed good to go. We were, at least physically, just fine. We were lucky. I was even luckier than some because my driver had arrived early and was patiently waiting to pick me up. Shortly after the plane careened off the runway, they closed the airport. No cars allowed in. Others had to spend the night, but I was able to go to my hotel. The roads were so bad on the way into the city that I could hardly sit still. I was jumpy. Nervous. Shell-shocked. I was not okay.

The next morning, I appeared on NBC's *Today* show, in the same clothes I'd flown in, because I still didn't have my luggage. People wanted to know what it was like; fascinated with that moment when you realize this might be the end. They wanted to know what I was thinking, sending a tweet right in the middle of it all. My only answer was, and still is, that I wasn't thinking logically. It was an impulsive decision, made out of fear. I wanted comfort from my community, connection to my friends. In that moment, I wasn't thinking of that blue check next to my name on Twitter and that every media outlet would pick it up. I was thinking of the fourteen people who tweet me every day, wanting them to know, wanting them to tell me it was all going to be okay.

Over fifty media outlets contacted me during that first hour after the crash landing. It was a frenzy. I guess I shouldn't be surprised—I'd inadvertently chummed the shark-infested media waters. There were even a disturbing number of people in the Twitterverse who were offended that I said "God is good." But He was. And He is.

When I finally got back to Birmingham, sent my "plane crash outfit" to the dry cleaner, and tried to get back to normal life, I was stuck for about a week—mentally and emotionally frozen in a state of suspended animation. Why did this happen to me? Faith is the most important thing in my life; I don't believe anything happens by accident. Such a near-miss: There had to be a reason.

In that moment, when all the events of my life flickered across my mind like scenes on film, I recognized that I had been living in the past. I was chasing a life that was, a life I used to have, and stubbornly refusing to sink in and love the life I have right now—the life that is. I had lived in Alabama for eight years, and for eight years my heels had been dug in deep. I'd spent most of my time looking back over my shoulder, longing for New Jersey and my life up north, quipping about southern eccentricities and putting Jersey on a pedestal. Not that Jersey doesn't deserve it. I love Jersey and I will always be a Jersey girl. But where had I been putting my energy and my focus? Into schemes for moving north, dragging my family along with me so I could relive my past? It had to stop.

I live in Alabama. There, I've said it. I live here right now, and this is my life, and if I don't fall in love with who I am here and where I am now and everything about the life I am living in this precious present moment, I have nothing. Life can be taken away so easily. You can lose it all in an instant. If you don't love it now, when will you start? When will it be too late?

This is my peace offering. This book I've been writing will be my love song to the South. This book is the story of my journey, and why I love where I came from, but how I learned to love where I am right here, right now. Because I do love it, and I have loved it, bit by bit, a little more each day, for years now. I just didn't want to admit it.

There is so much to love about the South. Sometimes it still seems strange to me. I don't always understand the customs, the language, the traditions, or the priorities. But I always understand that the South is filled with faith, and hope, and love. And that's what I want to be filled with, too.

So here it is—my take on life below the Mason-Dixon line. The Southern Education of the Jersey Girl. I hope you will join me in reaching across the border that divides us, to help create greater unity. Because in the end, in that final moment when you don't know whether you will live or die, what really matters?

Faith, hope, and love. And the greatest of these is love.

Part One

GOD BLESS THE BROKEN ROAD

We accept the love we think we deserve.

—STEPHEN CHBOSKY

Chapter 1

THE POWER OF A
GREAT PAIR OF JEANS

All roads lead to Michael. I've known it, or sensed it, almost from the beginning. But this particular road has been the longest, most winding road I've ever traveled that had sex at the end of it. Michael and I couldn't be more different. More than a decade apart in age, and even further apart in sensibility. Southern gentility versus Jersey brash. Soft-spoken versus loudmouth. Keep-it-to-yourself versus tell-the-world. Subtle versus out there. We were the Civil War incarnate. But somehow, it was never Michael versus me.

It was always me versus myself.

Have you ever taken yourself completely out of your natural environment and changed your life, willingly but with deep-seated reservations and against all common sense? Then you know something about the road I've traveled. This road has been riddled with potholes and detours and barren stretches of desert, as well as beauty and grandeur and serendipity and even inspiration. But to really understand the extremity of the journey, to get how completely Michael and everything he stands for transformed me from a lost soul into who I was meant to be all along— you must first understand who I was going into this journey.

I was twenty-six. I lived in my broken-in leather jacket and had long dark hair down to my butt. I was thin and tall and leggy and I was hot, and I loved loved loved my transient lifestyle. I was in PR, which is the perfect job for somebody like me. Somebody who was a runner.

That was me. A runner. A nomad. A girl without a home, who liked it that way. After a childhood of crazy highs and precipitous lows—a marginally Jewish childhood that included the significant influence of Italian Catholic grandparents and a culture largely made up of Italian Catholics and European Jews—I struggled to define myself. At seventeen years old, after the tragic death of my father, I left home to go to college, and I never came back for very long—just to breeze through to see the family. Then I was on my way again. I dabbled in the wild life and I loved it that way. Sometimes I was a bully. Sometimes I was a partier. Always, I worked to be the center of attention, but I was also quick on my feet, a people person, and I wasn't afraid to attack any problem head-on. When I entered the world of public relations, my job became the perfect excuse to stay on the move and avoid growing roots, making lasting connections, or getting too emotionally attached to anyone.

Because what did attachment involve, inevitably, but loss? Imagine building a great army of the strongest soldiers, but without a leader. That was me. I had weapons and shields and tons of strength, but no direction or accountability, or even a clear idea of what my war was about. I didn't have to know because I was too busy moving. Some people medicate, or drink, or eat to keep the fear down. I always kept one foot out the door. I never felt threatened or trapped because I always had an exit strategy, and the one thing that didn't scare me was walking away. I was never afraid to walk right out of someone's life, or walk right out of a job, because I didn't care. For me, being a nomad was about survival, and if you had asked me how that was working out for me, I would have told you, loud and clear and in the Jersey accent I was proud of, that I was just fine. Just fucking fine, thanks for asking.

So there I was, with my PR clients around the country, giving them everything I had. And my personal life? I had friends. I dated men. And even a few women. But if things weren't going well in New York, then oh well, I suddenly had to fly off to LA. When things got weird in LA, no problem, I'd run home to Jersey for a while. When that got oppressive, I'd hop on a plane and check up on the southeastern market. And by the time I was back in New York, things would have settled down. Whatever had gone sour was water under the bridge and I could start fresh. Find a new man. Find a new group of friends. Invent a new me.

The day I met Michael for the first time, I was in Birmingham, Alabama, to meet with the publisher of a local magazine. Considering all the exciting places I spent my time in, Birmingham wasn't my favorite spot in the world. However, it was where the magazine was based, and the publishers liked to touch base with me in person every so often. I was used to the big city, so Birmingham bored me, and I never made an effort to get to know much about it. Why should I? It was just so . . . so . . . *southern*. And I was a Yankee, through and through. I was a Jersey girl, and I liked Bon Jovi and Bruce Springsteen and fist pumping and disco fries. I was a club dancer and a fast talker and I made a mean lasagna. But work was work and so down south I went—it was an excuse to keep moving. I knew perfectly well that I was too cool for Alabama, and I exuded that in my attitude. (No wonder nobody talked to me.) I didn't try to make friends, beyond my client list. I made sure I didn't blend. God forbid I would be mistaken for a local! But once in a while, after a long meeting, a girl just needs a drink—even at the risk of interacting with the natives.

A colleague recommended a local café called Bottega, so I sidled in that evening, full of Jersey attitude, in my black leather jacket and my tight jeans and my red lipstick, flipping my long straight hair and conveying confidence. I slid onto a barstool and surveyed the drink menu. Twelve dollars for a cocktail? Who did these people think they were—New Yorkers? Although my life had its glamorous elements, a high salary wasn't one of them and twelve dollars was out of my budget. I scanned the room. The café was full of well-dressed, polite-seeming southerners. I knew from watching movies about the South that a real southern gentleman wouldn't let me pay for my own drink. So I slid off my stool, jutted out a hip, looked around the room, shifted just so in my jeans, and flipped my long hair.

Sure enough, a few minutes later the bartender placed a Manhattan in front of me. Not my drink of choice, but no matter, it was free. I looked around. A handsome southern gentleman raised his glass and smiled at me. He was cute, in an older-guy sort of way. (And by older, I mean he might have been forty.) I raised my glass back to him, stood up with my drink, and grabbed my purse, intending to thank him. As I was approaching him, I stumbled, putting a crimp in my attitude. I looked up and caught his eye. To me, he looked like a mix of Big from *Sex and the City* and Matthew McConaughey. Older . . . but hot. Definitely hot.

"Hi," I said. "Thanks for the drink."

"My pleasure," he said. "Have a seat." His voice was soft and strong, like orange blossom honey. God, where did I come up with such a metaphor? And yet there it was. Like honey. He was tanned and compact, trim but strong looking, with sandy hair and the most amazingly piercing light-blue eyes. I couldn't stop looking at those eyes. They contradicted his gentle manner, his laid-back posture, and his mild smile. *He's complicated*, I thought. *His eyes give him away.*

"So, my name's Jaime."

"You're not from here," he said. It wasn't a question.

"What gave me away?" I said, laughing.

"I guessed New York," he said, gesturing at the Manhattan. "But now that I hear you speak, I'd say New Jersey."

I smiled proudly. "Absolutely," I said. "But I have an apartment in New York. So you were half right."

I waited. Wasn't he going to tell me his name? He took a deep pull of his Scotch. I felt like he had the advantage. I had offered my name. I should have waited until he asked! It was a misstep that made me feel vulnerable. I didn't want to give in by asking him his name. I had to act like I didn't care to know.

"What do you do? Wait, let me guess. You're a businessman. An ethical businessman who honors the power of the handshake and opens doors for ladies and goes to church every Sunday and doesn't believe Alabama should be sullied by new-fangled debauchery like casinos or the lottery or medical marijuana, but you've got a case of Scotch in your basement and a gun rack in your truck."

He smiled. "You're half right," he said.

Maddening! "Which half?" I said, trying to fish without making it too obvious.

"I'm a state lobbyist for the alcohol and gaming industries."

"Oh." I was speechless. It wasn't what I expected. And I have to admit, his answer was a little exciting. Was he smirking at me? I blushed and flipped my hair, for courage. "So, you represent vice in the South."

"Basically," he said, taking another pull of his Scotch. Oh, he was smooth. And he had me off balance, which was both thrilling and aggravating. Not that it mattered. I had a boyfriend. A problematic boyfriend, a heartbreaking, soul-crushing boyfriend, but a boyfriend nevertheless. I finished my drink and stood up, extending my hand. "Look, I have to go, but it was really nice to meet you . . ."

"Michael," he said, taking my hand. His hands were warm and strong and clean. He squeezed. My heart skipped a beat. "May I call you?"

I smiled. And felt a pang of regret. "I'm with someone," I said.

"Well then," he said, his eyes meeting mine. "Good-bye, Jersey Jaime."

I turned, conscious that he was watching me walk away. I didn't flip my hair again (I mean, enough is enough already), but I stood straighter, taller. I knew he was interested, and that gave me confidence. For once, I decided that I didn't need to overdo it. I felt a little glow. In some way, I had met my match.

In the sea of southern men I encountered every time I was in town, southern men whom I found to be extraordinarily plain, here was somebody with flavor. When somebody can make you feel something in twenty minutes, you don't forget that.

And then I went back to New York.

I thought about him over the next few months. He wasn't my type at all. My type is the bad boy, the troublemaker, the rebel, the scrapper. The guy who needs to be fixed or who tries to fix me. My type is the guy with attitude. And by attitude, I mean Jersey attitude, not the proper, genteel, reserved attitude of a southern gentleman. And yet, that was Michael, and it made an impression.

I continued my nomadic ways. From Jersey to New York to the South to LA and back to New York, a perpetual carousel ride around the country. I was back in Birmingham often enough over the following year to finally make a few friends (in spite of myself). I told myself I needed people to hang out with while I was in town and there were, admittedly, some girls who knew how to have fun. The first was my hairstylist. Her name was Jenny and she was my age, and she liked to party. One night, she invited me to go out with her and some friends, and I accepted. That was when I met Leigh Anne.

As soon as I saw Leigh Anne, I felt like I was looking in a mirror. She was a single mom, but could easily have passed for a single non-mom, and we were fascinated with each other from the beginning because we looked so much alike. We both had the same tall, narrow-hipped build and the same long dark hair, and when we met, it was as if we'd known each other for years.

Leigh Anne came from Mississippi. Although she was a

southerner, she was also an outsider, so I forgave her. She was from a completely different kind of southern environment—the shit-kicking, gun-toting, cowboy-boot-wearing Deep South. That made more sense to me than subdued and etiquette-conscious Birmingham. Leigh Anne didn't seem like a southern belle to me. She had certain southern characteristics—she was warm and polite. But I also loved that she never made me feel awkward or wrong or like I didn't belong, and that brought my guard down. I love other women easily, and I loved her immediately. Basically, Leigh Anne was the kind of friend with whom I could exchange *I love you*s by our third meeting, and no matter how bad the storm raged in either of our lives, Leigh Anne was the one who could always laugh about it.

She was also funky and eclectic. She wore hippie clothes without being a hippie and changed up her accessories in the coolest ways. (Like most commitments, a commitment to creative accessorizing is one I have never been able to make, but I always admire it in others.) And she was the first one who defended the South to me, rather than not caring or even asking how I felt about it. She told me that there was more to the South than my preconceptions, and also much more than I could ever know from Birmingham alone. "Birmingham is just a small piece of the South," she would say. "The South is full of surprises." And so was she, from her cowboy hat to her shit-kicking boots to her perfect, perfect boobs.

One day, she invited me over to her home for coffee. As she talked, I couldn't help staring. She was wearing a white button-down blouse, and I had to ask. "Are your boobs fake?"

"Yes." She said it without hesitation or shame.

"Can I see them?"

"Sure," she said, and opened up her shirt. They were . . . spectacular.

"Fuck. I want boobies like that," I said.

"Touch them before you decide you want to make a purchase. And wait until after you have babies," she warned.

"Babies," I said, laughing. I touched. "They feel weird. But good weird. I could deal with that. Will you come with me for my consultation?"

I didn't end up going through with it. That *babies* comment stuck in the back of my mind like a splinter, so I told myself I would wait. There was no hurry. But if I had done it, I would have dragged Leigh Anne along with me, pointed to her, and said, *Doc, give me a pair of those.*

It was Leigh Anne and Jenny and a few other fun girls who were with me a year after the first time I met Michael, when I encountered him again.

It had to have been fate—one of those encounters you can't avoid because it's going to happen no matter what you do. That's how it felt to me, at least. I was newly single, having finally escaped from the soul-crushing boyfriend. I had just flown in from New York for meetings with the magazine, and I was out with the girls at Bottega, the same café where I had met Michael almost a year before. We were drinking and being rowdy and the place was about to close. I was sitting on Leigh Anne's lap when he walked through the door.

I meet thousands of people in my line of work, and I can't possibly remember them all, but I remembered him. I didn't just recognize him, I *remembered* him. There is a difference.

"Hey, I know that guy!" I said.

"That's Michael Sullivan," said Jenny.

"You know him?"

"Of course. Everybody knows him," she said. "He's one of those 'Most Eligible Bachelor' guys. No wife, no kids."

"No way." I stared at her. "Are you serious?"

"He's super cute," Leigh Anne said. "But super old."

"Yeah," I said, distracted. "Hey, will you guys excuse me for a minute?"

"You're not," said Jenny.

"Wanna bet?" I said. I scooted off Leigh Anne's lap and vamped my way over to him.

"Hey there!" I said. "Remember me?"

"Heeeeyyyy!" he said, grinning . . . Wait, grinning? This wasn't the mild-mannered smile or the carefully self-controlled man I'd encountered before. It didn't take me long to realize he'd had a few drinks.

"Whoa, buddy," I said as he swayed in front of me. "You all right there?"

"I never forgot you," he said. He seemed to realize his condition. He took my hand—a bold gesture for him, clearly. "I'm sorry. I've been playing golf in the sun all day. And drinking vodka."

"Say no more," I said. "We've all been there."

"Bartender!" he said, leaning on the bar. "This lady would like a Manhattan." He turned to me. "You would like a Manhattan, wouldn't you?"

"Actually, a Cosmo would be nicer," I said.

"Strike that!" he said, raising his hand. "Make it a Cosmo! And a pizza to go."

"Sure thing, Sully," said the bartender.

He turned and looked me up and down. "You look good," he said.

"Thanks," I said. "So do you. You know, for an old guy."

He laughed. So he could take a joke.

I turned. Leigh Anne and Jenny were staring at us, wide-eyed and openmouthed. I waved and pointed at Michael. Jenny nodded. Leigh Anne made a hand gesture like, *Go, go!*

We sat at the bar and talked and drank while he waited for his pizza, and he flirted more openly than he had before. He was definitely older than anyone I'd ever dated. I quickly realized that his temporarily loose-lipped state was my chance to score more information, and I found out that (a) he was thirteen years older than me; (b) his parents lived in town and he was one of five boys; and (c) even when drunk, he was a true southern gentleman—still extremely polite and respectful. My interest was piqued. I had to find out more about what this guy was all about. Why wasn't he married? What about him made him so "eligible"? And most of all, why was I getting that fluttery feeling around him? This guy gave me butterflies, and not the typical stomach butterflies. I'm talking vagina butterflies. It wasn't like me to feel this way. It wasn't like me at all.

When he stood up to leave, he swayed again and I took matters into my own hands. "I'm driving you home," I said.

"No, no," he said, waving a hand. "I can walk."

"Nope," I said. "It's decided." I waved to Leigh Anne and Jenny and then drove him home in my car. He fell asleep in the passenger seat, although his head never lolled forward like a drunkard. His eyes simply closed, and he began to snore lightly.

It was a gentlemanly snore if I ever heard one. I could have been insulted that he fell asleep in my presence, but instead I felt protective. When we got to the address he had given me after finally agreeing that I could drive him home, I pulled up in the driveway and peered through the gloom at the shadowy house. A bachelor's house. Larger than you would expect, a putting green in the front yard and a beautiful porch both neat and well kept. The windows were dark. "Good morning, sunshine!" I said. Without a word, he opened the car door, got out, and walked slowly and in a perfectly straight line to the door, his keys ready. He didn't even turn back to wave.

"You're welcome," I muttered, and drove back to my small, temporary apartment near the magazine offices. I didn't know what to make of the encounter. Was he too drunk to remember to say good night? Was he embarrassed? Was he pretending it wasn't happening? I had no idea whether he would remember in the morning, or if I would ever see him again. It was a strange good-bye, definitely not what I'd expected. I felt a little deflated, and my first instinct was the usual one: moving on. I couldn't wait to get to LA. I had a flight out in less than a week.

But two days later, he called me. He said he had begged the bartender to track down my number. He apologized for his behavior in a most gentlemanly manner, and asked if I was free to accompany him to dinner the following night. I was surprised at how happy I was to hear from him. I agreed to meet him (although why wasn't he offering to pick me up?). We met at a little Italian restaurant whose food is legendary for sending women into labor. So there we were, a couple on our first date, surrounded by women who were nine months' pregnant and scarfing down lasagna (which in itself is a curiosity in the South) at a rapid pace. The beauty of this was that I was definitely the skinniest chick in the room.

We talked about everything. He talked about things most people don't talk about on a first date—politics and religion and how he grew up going to Catholic school and what kind of mother he had. I was fascinated. It felt easy to be with him. I remember at one point telling him a story about my mother. When I talk about my mother, I tend to slip immediately into her New York accent and demeanor, which is definitely different from mine—she's like me times ten. Halfway through the story, I noticed that Michael was almost staring through me with this little smirk on his face.

"What?" I said, stopping the story. "What, do I have a booger? Do I have something in my teeth?"

"No, I'm just listening," he said, leaning back in his chair.

"But you're staring at me!"

"No, I'm watching you," he said. "But look around. Everybody else is staring."

I looked around and he was right. Everybody was staring at me.

"Oh my God," I said in a Jersey whisper (which is much louder than a southern whisper). "Am I totally embarrassing you?"

"No, not at all," he said. "I've just never seen anybody like you."

Slipping into my best Joe Pesci accent, I said, "Oh, I'm funny? I'm funny how, I mean funny like I'm a clown? I amuse you?" He hadn't seen *Goodfellas*, so he didn't get it. He just raised his eyebrows at me. "Never mind," I said.

After dinner he walked me to my car and opened the door for me. Of course, being twenty-seven years old and very tristate, I was like, "Dude, I can open my own car door!"

He just laughed. "You're relentless," he said.

That night, back at my temporary apartment, I fell onto the couch, picked up the phone, and called my mom.

"Ma, I have good news and bad news," I said. "The good news is, I just had dinner with the man I'm pretty sure I'm going to marry. The bad news is that he lives in Birmingham, Alabama."

#cawfeetawk

So often we bypass people because they don't fit our preconceived notions of what we think we want. What really connects us to one another is a feeling—a feeling that calls us to truly see the person in front of us and be moved by how they make us feel. Call it chemistry, call it the recognition that we have met someone we can appreciate for who they are, rather than wishing they were something they're not. Whatever it is, it is worth paying attention to. The ones you end up loving the most might not be at all who you thought they would be.

Chapter 2

BREAKING UP IS EASY

You know the girl who goes on a date and finds herself obsessively thinking about the person and constantly checking her phone to see if he called? I had always misunderstood, even mocked, the energy of that girl. Yet I became that girl. Michael was the man for me, I was sure of it. I had decided that someday, somehow, I would marry him. He was curiously reserved, unquestionably southern, but rugged and sexy, soft-spoken and intelligent. He was my exact opposite—and husband material all the way. He had a real job. He was a real man. I wasn't used to dating real men. I was used to dating boys disguised as men acting like boys. It was new and novel and sexy.

And so we began our courtship. But dating Michael Sullivan, alleged Most Eligible Bachelor in Birmingham, proved challenging and incredibly confusing for me. He didn't kiss me on the first date. Fine. He was a gentleman. But when you're dating someone, you wait after each date for that moment. Is it going to happen this time? Is he going to kiss me? And if not by the second date, surely by the third date. Am I right? By the third date, I always thought you should be sleeping together, if it's going really well.

Apparently, that's not how they do things in Alabama.

The dates went on. Every time, he called me to see if I was free, and if I was, he would choose the place, and ask me to meet him there. He never picked me up. I never picked him up. He never invited me over. And after every date, he would say a fond and polite good-bye as he helped me into my car . . . but never a kiss. First date, second date, third date, fourth. They were always the same. I was making more excuses to spend more time in Birmingham, as it had suddenly and improbably become more interesting to me than New York or LA, but he never saw me more than once a week, and he always called me. I never called him.

You might be wondering why a take-charge gal like myself didn't call him (not to mention take matters into my own hands and just kiss him). The strange thing was, Michael led the dating process from the very beginning. He set the tone. I'd never experienced anything like it. I was used to setting the tone. I suppose I could have called him, and I considered it frequently, but something always held me back. Sometimes I would go out with a girlfriend for a drink, catch a buzz, and dial his number, but I could never press SEND. I just couldn't do it. We had something going, and I didn't want to destroy the rhythm and magic of it. I could tell he liked chasing me and, what's more, liked that I wasn't chasing him. For some reason, I was willing to play along. This was weird because I don't let anyone lead. Even as a kid, when I took horseback riding lessons, I would purposefully make my horse trot past the teacher.

"Jaime! Fall in line!" he would yell.

"No way, bitches!" (Okay, I didn't actually *say* that, but that's what I was thinking, all the way.) When the riding instructor called my mom, she said, "What do you want me to tell you? She doesn't fall in line at home, either."

So why was I falling in line with this older man's strange southern custom of moving at a snail's pace? I came to look forward to him opening my door, asking me on dates, pulling out my chair for me. At the same time, it was disconcerting. I felt like one of Charlie's Angels, never knowing when I was going to get that call and what it might involve. On the dates, he was polite, attentive, funny, and often stayed silent, just listening to me talk. He genuinely seemed to enjoy this. He told me I looked beautiful. He always picked up the check. He was the perfect gentleman. But there was no lip locking. As if kissing was somehow inappropriate or vulgar. In Jersey, kissing is pretty much at the level of a handshake, so I really didn't understand the holdup. Was there something wrong with me? Why wasn't he dying to plant one on me? Not to mention, why wasn't he dying to have sex? Because when you haven't even kissed, sex seems like it's a million miles away.

So occasionally I went out with other guys, and I knew that he sometimes went out with other girls. He was always my first choice. I would accept an invitation with Michael over an invitation from any other man.

Sometimes I had to ask myself, *What is this guy's game?* What was his motivation? I checked my breath after every date. Was I somehow repelling him? I questioned my judgment. I was young and he was old—a mature man in his forties from a completely different culture. How did I know this wasn't the way it was supposed to go? Maybe this was how old people dated. Maybe people in their twenties had sex after the third date, but people in their forties went to the early-bird special and never kissed. Who was I to say he was wrong and I was right?

But a girl can only remain unkissed for so long. We started dating in August, and in October, Michael forgot my birthday.

I was celebrating my birthday at a strip club called Sammy's. Don't judge. Strip clubs are fun, and . . . well, if you want to dance at a club in Birmingham, the strip club is your only option. I was there with all my girlfriends, but I was distracted. I knew Michael and I weren't exclusive. I knew we hadn't even kissed. But *how could he forget my birthday?* Isn't that one of those things the first-choice man in your life is obligated to remember? Honestly, the fact that I had nothing but radio silence from Michael on my birthday brought on a tidal wave of insecurities. Maybe I didn't mean as much to him as he meant to me. Maybe he was with another woman he liked more than he liked me. Maybe he was a careless person. (I knew that wasn't true.) While one part of me chastised myself for making a big deal about it, the other half wailed and whined and self-pitied, and eventually got angry.

I remember sitting in the corner while some woman was shaking her pasties in my face when my anger got the best of me. I grabbed my cell phone and dialed his number. The phone rang. I put one finger in my ear and Michael answered.

"Hello?" he said, as if he hadn't a care in the world.

"Hi," I said. It was a greeting clipped and edged with venom, but hey, I was pissed off.

"How are you?" he said, hesitantly.

"I'm good, how are you?" I said.

"Just fine," he said. Then—nothing. He'd forgotten. It was confirmed.

"Just so you know, it's my birthday," I said. Why mince words? There was silence on the line. "And just so you know," I continued, "don't call me again." I hung up on him.

Extreme? Maybe. But this is the part of a relationship where I typically get scared (or bored) and break it off anyway, so this was my grand opportunity to follow my dysfunctional pattern. I mean, really, he hadn't even kissed me yet, and how long was I going to let him string me along like that? And Alabama? What was I thinking? Clearly he was all wrong for me. The major obstacles in our way greatly overshadowed any initial notion I had had about our chemistry. Chemistry. Ha! How ridiculous. I was so much better off without him! I felt cleansed as I turned off my phone and slipped it into my purse. I looked at the stripper in front of me. "How *you* doin'?" My friends guffawed and I grinned and got up to dance, but I felt sadder than I thought I should have felt at that moment. There I was, surrounded by a great group of friends and hardworking pole dancers, and I was mooning over a *man*? So pathetic.

After a week, I still hadn't heard anything. Another week passed. The holidays came and went, and though I still thought about him, I assumed our time together was over. If he'd missed *Thanksgiving*, well then . . . he must have moved on to more southern pastures. I was in town sporadically—off to New York, off to LA, the usual routine. I went home to Jersey for Christmas. After that, I had to be back in Alabama for meetings. I arrived feeling dull and listless. Alabama held little charm for me now, but at least I had friends. I called Leigh Anne, and she agreed to go to a movie with me. I met her at the theater, we got popcorn, and we sat down. That's when my phone vibrated.

It was a text message from Michael. The first in over two months.

The text contained just four words: *Are you in town?* I didn't know if I wanted to jump up and down and scream, *Yes, yes, YES!* or if I wanted to throw my phone at the screen. I briefly considered texting back, *New phone. Who dis?* But I just couldn't do it, so I opted for brevity. I sent back one word: *Yes.*

Say more by saying less. It was true, it was to-the-point, and it was unemotional. It couldn't possibly get me in trouble.

He texted back: *I left something on your porch. I hope to hear from you soon.*

It took me about five seconds to kiss Leigh Anne on the forehead and hightail it out of that movie theater. What could it be? *What could he have left on my porch?* I was dying. *Dying.* I drove home as fast as I could and I ran up to my porch. There was a bag. I opened my front door, ran upstairs to my apartment, and opened the bag. It was the most recent season of *Sex and the City* on DVD. He wrote something on the card like, *I screwed up. I'm sorry.* SO big of him.

It was the peace offering of all peace offerings. "Just DVDs?" you say? To me, that gift represented everything I could ever want in a man. Michael could never have known what *Sex and the City* really meant to me—that nothing in the world brought me as much joy and entertainment as this show. Michael didn't know Carrie Bradshaw from Carrie Fisher. I imagined him parking his car at the store and walking in and asking somebody if they could help him find the *Sex and the City* DVDs. To most people, that would be nothing, but I knew this man and I knew that even though he knew nothing about my world, he knew it was important to me. He knew because he listened to me. I held out the DVDs in front of me. That's what it was really all about: *He listened to me.* It wasn't about getting a present. It wasn't about getting to watch the DVDs, even. *He was paying attention.* All my doubts, anger, and justifications for dumping him dissolved.

I called him.

"Thank you so much," I said. "You can't know what this means to me."

"I'm glad," he said. "I really am very sorry."

I had no impulse to refuse his apology. Michael isn't the kind of man you browbeat. When he apologizes, he means it wholeheartedly.

"I'd like to make it up to you," he said. "Can I take you out to dinner? We'll celebrate your birthday."

I thought about it for two seconds. "Only if I get to pick the place," I said.

"Of course. Anywhere you want to go."

Cut to Michael and me, sitting at a hibachi table surrounded by an assortment of Alabama's finest, with Japanese people banging gongs with a pineapple boat and singing happy birthday to me. I picked the place, all right. Michael doesn't really go to chain restaurants. He's kind of a foodie, so if I was going to choose, I was going to make it count. *This* would be his penance. Michael wanted to die but he refused to let me know it. When we walked out to the parking lot afterward, I couldn't help myself.

"Wasn't that great?" I said, feeling as happy as I ever had.

"I'll tell you this much," he said. "I'll never forget your birthday again."

#cawfeetawk

Sometimes well-intentioned people still hurt us. It doesn't mean they are bad people. We all say and do things we shouldn't sometimes. Or we fail to say and do things for those we love. Accepting a sincere apology and letting it go is the healthiest thing we can do. Not for them, but for ourselves.

Chapter 3

THE KISS EXPERIMENT

𝒩ew Year's Day came and went, and yet he still hadn't kissed me. I stopped expecting it after a while, but it still needled me. We were still both dating other people at this point. We hadn't had the "exclusive" conversation, so this was understood, even if undeclared. I wasn't enjoying dating around as much as I used to. I was dating other people more because I could, not because I wanted to. Whenever I was on a date with another guy and he would kiss me good night, I would find myself wondering why Michael hadn't, and wishing it was Michael kissing me instead.

I really wanted to understand this kissing issue, because damn it, I liked this guy. A lot. And I also like kissing a lot. It's intimate and important, and moves the relationship forward. And while I was willing to hold off to some degree, I wasn't going to buy a lemon. If there was some major weird issue under the surface, I had to know. So I decided to conduct an experiment. Was it just Michael, or was this really a southern thing? Normally when I dated, it was in the other cities I frequented, but when a cute southern guy at a BBQ joint asked me on a date, I accepted.

We went on your standard date, and afterward he walked me to my door. Sensing a moment of awkwardness, I said, "Are you going to kiss me?"

He looked surprised. "If you want me to," he said.

"Were you going to kiss me if I hadn't said anything?" I pressed him.

"No, probably not."

"Why the hell not?"

"Well, I don't know," he stammered. "Because it's our first date, and I just wouldn't feel . . . I don't know . . ." He held out his hands in a gesture of retreat and surrender.

Interesting. He was totally taken aback that I had asked him that question. So maybe it wasn't just Michael. Maybe it was *all southern men*. I pushed him further.

"Okay, let's say we really hit it off and we started dating regularly. At what point would you go for the kiss?" I said.

He looked like a cornered animal. "Uhh . . . I don't know . . . it depends on the situation. It depends on . . . where it's going?" He said it as a question and looked to me for confirmation that he had it right.

"What the fuck is wrong with you people?" I blustered. "If you had a nice time, and you think you want to see someone again, and you're attracted to her, and she had a nice time, what's the problem? It's a kiss. It's just a kiss!"

"So you . . . you . . . you want me to kiss you?" he said. Clearly, the very idea now terrified him.

"Oh, forget it," I said, and shut the door in his face.

Southern Wisdom

Southern men want to be sure you want to be kissed before they kiss you. Northern men don't care if you want to be kissed. If they want to kiss you, they will try to kiss you.

Now I needed to test my theory in a more forward-thinking city. The next week, I went on a date with a guy in New York. He took me to a trendy place that was loud and bustling with beautiful people. He asked how I liked Birmingham, and then, "What are the guys like in Alabama? Do they take you out for grits and iced tea?" He snorted.

I surprised myself by getting defensive. "As a matter of fact," I said, "I'm dating a guy there and he is respectful and smart and charming and he smells like vanilla cupcakes and I literally want to rub one out four times a week when we're apart."

"Okay . . ." the guy said, rolling his eyes at me. I found myself thinking, *Fucking New Yorkers, they're all so cynical.*

"So, let me ask you something," I said. "What is your criteria to kiss a girl good night after a date?"

"What do you mean?" he said, sipping his metrosexual martini with interest.

"Like, say you are on a date with a girl. What would determine whether or not you kissed her at the end of the night? What is your kiss-worthy criterion?"

"Hotness," he said without hesitation. "Why? Are you wondering whether you qualify?"

Gross.

Suddenly, I saw this guy sitting across from me for all the things he was that I didn't want anymore, and I thought, *What the fuck am I doing?* I didn't want to be here with this guy, or any other guy. So Michael hadn't kissed me. So what? Could I live without kissing? No, probably not. But I had to believe it was coming. The kiss was in the making. The long . . . slow . . . snail's-pace making. The kiss was coming, and I had to believe that. The guy across from me was scanning the club to see who else he might know, maybe sensing my waning interest in him and his cocky northern ways. He was no Michael Sullivan. That was for sure. I could only hope that maybe Michael was somewhere out there, sitting at a table with a woman, wishing she was me.

At the end of the date, the guy did try to kiss me, and I stopped him. I thought about all the men in New York and LA and New Jersey who had tried to kiss me, and all the times I had allowed it, even when I didn't really want it. Why would I do that? I was beginning to understand what I wanted. And it wasn't this . . . this . . . this life of *extraneous kissing*! I wanted a real kiss. I wanted a kiss that mattered. And I wanted it from Michael.

Then New York happened, throwing everything I thought I'd figured out into doubt again.

#cawfeetawk

How often do we form habits that satisfy our ego but little more? Sure, it's nice to know somebody wants to kiss you, but is it worth kissing them back and sending yourself in the wrong direction? Kissing somebody I didn't really want to kiss was one habit I was happy to break. I wish I'd done it years before.

– *Chapter 4* –

"HONEY, HE'S GAY"

That February, Michael was in New York for work, and I also happened to be in the city for work. He was staying at a hotel, and I suggested we get together. I was excited to see him outside of Birmingham. In five months I'd never once seen him wearing anything but a suit. I didn't know if the man owned a pair of jeans, because every time we'd been together it was for some formal thing like a nice dinner date or church.

Jersey Whispers

Regarding church: Yes, southern people go on dates to church. It's a thing. Second: This man was so genteel and socially appropriate that on our church date, when somebody two rows behind us farted, he refused to laugh! I was cracking up. I could not stop laughing. My eyes were watering and he literally looked at me and said, "You're so irreverent." That was just the first of many comments regarding my inappropriate behavior I've gotten from him over the years, but I'm sorry, it was fucking funny. If you can't laugh at a fart in church, what can you laugh at? And really, *I'm* irreverent? I wasn't the person letting one rip in the house of God.

He asked me to meet him at his hotel, so the first thing I thought was: *Hotel? Are we going to have sex? Are we finally going to have sex?!* I couldn't believe it. Clearly, he had planned this all along. He was waiting until we were somewhere romantic, and he would sweep me off my feet, and it would be like a movie. To make things even more picturesque, it was snowing that day. What I didn't realize was how much this snow would impact our entire New York experience.

As I went down to the corner to get a cab to his hotel, the snow started falling harder and faster. Cars were sliding down the street, and there were hardly any cabs. "This isn't going to be romantic if I die in a horrible taxi crash," I said to myself. I tried to hail a cab but every cab I saw slid right past me. Finally one pulled up carefully to the curb and I slipped and skated and basically somehow managed to catapult myself into the backseat. I got myself together, brushing off the snow, and we fishtailed all the way down First Avenue as the snow got thicker and heavier. "I'm gonna die," I muttered to myself. "I'm finally on my way to have sex with this gorgeous, sexy, actual adult man, and I'm never going to get there because I'm gonna die."

But I didn't die. Somehow, we got to the hotel, I stumbled out of the cab and slipped along the pavement to the door, attempting to maintain a modicum of grace as I careened past the doorman. I found Michael's floor and suddenly felt nervous—that familiar nervous pre-sex-for-the-first-time thrill. I fixed my hair. I adjusted my clothes. I pinched my cheeks and pressed my lips together. I walked toward his room, imagining what he would look like with his shirt off. How he would approach me? What he would whisper? *This is it*, I thought to myself. *I've waited for so long!* I was practically swooning.

But he came out of his room, shut the door behind him, and met me halfway down the hallway. It was almost like he was afraid to let me near the door.

I stopped, confused and disappointed. *Okay, fine*, I thought. *We'll do it his way. He can wine and dine me first.* Then *we'll have sex.* Only then did I notice that he was wearing jeans and a sweater. Damn, he looked good in those Levi's. "I've never seen you out of a suit!" I said.

"I guess you haven't," he said in his sexy southern drawl. I waited. It was the perfect setup for a comment full of innuendo. Something like, *You'll see me out of these jeans by the end of the night, baby.* But nothing. Nada. He put his hand on the small of my back to guide me back to the elevator. Either he was being so subtle that it completely escaped me, or sex wasn't even on his radar. How could that be?

We stepped out into the snowpocalypse.

New York doesn't shut down for anything, but this was different. This was the biggest snowstorm I could ever remember hitting the city. It was brutal. The snow was coming down in curtains, obliterating the tops of the buildings, falling into our eyelashes, sticking all over our coats. We wandered through Midtown and I'd never seen anything like it—it was a ghost town. I grew up fifty minutes from the city, and this was unheard of. It was strange and exciting to be the only ones walking through the streets of Manhattan in the snow. I was glad I was with Michael. I held his arm and hugged it close. I felt safe. And hungry.

But everything was closed. Restaurant after restaurant was dark and shuttered. The stores were closed, even the delis. Finally we turned a corner and saw an OPEN sign. We ducked inside and the manager came forward.

"We're closing," she said. "But if you want to order right now, we can get you something from a limited menu. Here's what we've got."

"We'll take it," I said.

We sat down, the only customers in the dimly lit room with red-and-white-checked tablecloths and wooden furniture and a row of wine bottles and candles along a ledge in front of the kitchen. Michael ordered a bottle of wine and we both ordered pasta. "We need carbs!" I said. "Snowstorms are strenuous," then gave him a wink. As we ate, they shut down the restaurant around us, stacking chairs on the tables, cleaning the bar, glancing at us as they hovered around the register, trying to close it out. They gave us the check in the middle of our dinner, but we weren't in a hurry. I savored the moment—the two of us together, alone in the storm, Michael holding my hand across the table. The only romantic thing we didn't do was share a piece of spaghetti, à la *Lady and the Tramp*. I felt a little dizzy from the wine and the cold and the perfection of it all. We watched the snow through the plate-glass window, we talked, we laughed, we exclaimed about the weather. *I'm so in love with you!* I thought to myself. I didn't dare say it, of course. When we were finished, Michael put his napkin on the table, stood up, and said, "All right, let's find you a cab."

Oy vey.

Really, with the sending me home again? After all the wine and snowy romance? All my romantic feelings disappeared and

I was angry. *All right, then*, I thought. *If that's how he wants to play it, he can put me in that cab and then he can try to call me later and I may or may not ever answer the phone again.* I was ready to storm off through the storm, to slam the cab door, to glare at him as I drove away . . . but there was a glitch in my plan, and his. There was not a cab in sight.

In fact, there was nothing in sight. No cabs, no trucks, no cars, no nothing. The streets were deserted. Suddenly the snow didn't seem quite so romantic. It was colder, icier, slushier, and more miserable than before. Obviously thrown off his game and uncharacteristically unsure of himself, Michael looked up one direction of the deserted whiteout and down the other. "There will be a cab in front of my hotel," he said. "Let's walk."

We slogged back through the blizzard-buried streets like it was the final scene of *The Shining*. By the time we saw the hotel up ahead, the tips of my fingers were numb and my toes felt frozen inside my boots. We approached the doorman, who was huddled inside the foyer. "Can you hail us a cab?" he asked.

He looked at us like we were crazy. "I'm sorry, sir, but I haven't seen a cab in over an hour. It's gonna be a while."

I looked at Michael. Michael looked at the doorman. The doorman looked at me. I saw an opening. "Hey, buddy, let me ask you a question," I said to the doorman. Michael looked at me nervously. "If you were him right now, in this blizzard, in front of your hotel, and you couldn't get a cab, would you send me home, or would you take me upstairs to your room?"

The doorman looked me up and down. "Hell, no, I wouldn't send you home!" he said. "I'd be taking a fine young lady like you *right* upstairs."

A-ha! Checkmate. "Damn straight," I said.

Michael was blushing furiously because there just isn't a well-mannered southern response to an exchange like that. What could he do but agree? He shrugged helplessly. "All right," he said. "We'll go upstairs and see what the weather's gonna do." I grinned and tried to recall my morning underwear choice. We took the elevator, and I edged closer to him. I noticed that he edged slightly away. I followed him down the long hallway. I thought, *Here we go!*

Michael fumbled with the key card for a moment and opened the door. It was a nice Midtown hotel, and I noticed that even though he was only in New York for thirty-six hours, he had unpacked his entire suitcase. I opened the drawers and there were all his clothes, neatly folded. Even his underwear.

"What are you doing?" he said, looking embarrassed again as I inspected his things.

"Oh, this is *very nice. Very neat*," I said, thinking about the carnage that was my typical hotel room. I live out of my suitcase. For a second, it occurred to me how drastically different we really were. I shrugged. Opposites attract, right? I opened the wardrobe where he had just hung our coats. Melting snow dripped from our coat sleeves. He was looking more and more uncomfortable.

"Do you want a drink?" he said.

"God yes!" I said, thinking, *Let's get this machine lubricated!* He took out a little bottle of whiskey from the mini bar for himself, and a little bottle of white wine for me. He poured our drinks into the water glasses from the bathroom.

"This weather is . . . unprecedented," he said, awkwardly,

sitting in the upholstered chair under the reading lamp and crossing his legs. I could tell he was not prepared to have me in his personal space. I'd never been in his personal space before. I'd never even been inside his house, and here I was in his hotel room. From his point of view, I could see it might be . . . disconcerting.

"I love how you unpacked everything," I said sincerely, then sprawled on the bed suggestively. "Are you really this neat? *Everywhere?*" He could take that however he wanted, but apparently he didn't want to take it at all. He stayed rooted in his chair, clutching his glass of Scotch. Neither of us knew what to say next, so we both looked at the snow sticking to the window and blowing in flurries against the dark sky. We had separate flights back to Birmingham the next day, and it didn't take long for us both to be alerted, with subsequent beeps on our phones, that our flights had been canceled. Obviously, I was spending the night. I began to fear that the situation might give Michael an *actual heart attack.*

Finally, Michael got up, turned on the TV, and went back to his chair. But I was patient. I would wait him out. He would have to get into the bed at some point. The later it got, the less he would be able to deny it. I ran my tongue over my teeth. I had no toothbrush, no change of clothes, no hair brush, no pajamas. Everything was at the small apartment I kept in the city. But no matter. At least I was going to have sex. Once we were both in bed under the covers together, what else could possibly happen?

When it was almost midnight and I was afraid Michael was going to doze off in his chair, I decided somebody had to take some action. "Okay, I'm sleeping in my underwear because I've got nothing else," I said. I slowly pulled my shirt off and unzipped my pants, wiggling out of them.

He kept his eyes on the window as he said, "I have a T-shirt you can sleep in." He stood up, opened a drawer, and tossed a perfectly folded white T-shirt onto the bed.

"Gee . . . thanks?" I said.

Then he said something like, "Now, don't try to touch me tonight." He said it playfully, but I could also tell he was dead serious.

"Eww, get over yourself," I said, trying not to show my disappointment. "Nobody's touching you." He laughed. "Loser," I muttered.

Finally, he went into the bathroom and came out in . . . pajamas. Real pajamas. With long sleeves and long pants. I sighed loudly. He grabbed the remote, flipped to some stupid guy movie with car chases and explosions, and climbed into bed. I noticed he was practically perched on the edge, physically warning me not to try to snuggle, eyes glued to the television. We both stared at the movie, but I kept watching him out of the corner of my eye, waiting, mentally *willing him* to make a move. Surely, now that we were in bed together, his resolve would crumble and he wouldn't be able to keep his hands off me. I watched his hands. Would one of them creep across the bed? Would he roll over casually and drape an arm around me? Would he jump on me unexpectedly and ravish me?

And the answer is . . . none of the above. When the movie ended, he shut the TV off. "Good night, Jaime," he said, and rolled over. In the other direction.

"Good night, Michael," I said. I remember lying there in the dark thinking, *What the fuck? Is this a joke? Is this really happening right now? Do I need a hanky-panky check?*

So Jersey

In case you're not familiar with it, the hanky-panky check is where you put your hands in your underwear and then you smell your fingers to make sure you are not the problem.

I did a hanky-panky check, and I was fine. I had no issues, so clearly the issue was his. How was this handsome, full-blooded American male lying there in bed with a young attractive woman, sound asleep? As if to prove his total lack of arousal, he started snoring. I was completely baffled. I knew he liked me. It was obvious. And he knew I liked him. I'd made that pretty damn obvious, too. I felt confused and completely rejected.

The next morning, I woke up super early. Michael was still asleep. I looked out the window. The snow was finally letting up, spitting in icy droplets. I went into the bathroom and called my mom.

"Mom!" I said, trying not to be too Jersey loud. "I'm in his hotel room."

"You're in his hotel room?" she yelled back. I held the phone away from my ear. "Oh my gawd! You finally had sex!"

"No!" I Jersey-whispered. "He didn't even kiss me. He didn't even touch me!"

"Aye-aye-aye, I knew it!" She paused for dramatic effect. "Honey, he's gay. I knew it the whole time."

I sighed. "He's not gay, Ma."

"He's gay. Could it be more obvious? No straight man sleeps in bed with my gorgeous daughter and doesn't have sex with her."

"Aww, Mom, I love you. But he's not gay."

"He's a very nice, gentlemanly southern homosexual." She emphasized each syllable, like *ho-mo-SEK-shoo-al*. "Trust me, honey. A mother knows these things."

"All right," I conceded. "Maybe he's gay, but then why does he keep hanging out with me?"

"Some women have an attraction factor. It's like catnip for gay men. They like them, but they don't want to sleep with them. They want to *be them*."

I was not prepared to accept this, but it's pointless to argue with my mother.

"All right, Ma. Thanks. I love you. Bye!"

So Jersey

In Jersey, it is totally normal to talk in detail about your sex life to your mother.

I hung up the phone, went back into the room, and climbed back into bed, in that quiet-but-loud way you do when you want somebody to wake up but you don't want to be blamed for officially waking them up. I propped myself up on the pillows and crossed my arms. I was ready for a confrontation. He stirred, turned over, and stretched.

"Want coffee," he mumbled.

"My mom thinks you're gay."

"Good morning to you, too," he said with a half smile, swinging his legs over the side of the bed to sit up.

"Look, it's fine if you are," I said to his back. "But it would be nice to know. So I'm not, you know, wasting my time."

"I'm not gay," he said calmly, stretching his arms overhead.

"I don't mind if you are," I reassured him.

"I know," he said. "But I'm not."

"All right, then, whatever. I'm done trying to figure you out, so I'm just going to get back in the snow and walk the forty-seven blocks back to my apartment."

"No, no, I'll get you a cab," he said, in the most gentle-manly manner, especially considering I'd just questioned his sexual preference. He grabbed his clothes and went into the bathroom to get dressed. I flopped back down into the pillows. Hopeless!

He walked me downstairs, got me a cup of coffee, hailed me a cab, gave the cabdriver cash, and sent me on my way. On the cab ride back to my apartment, as we drove through the city and I watched New York coming back to life, I thought, *Was everything shut down last night, including me?* It was one of the strangest nights of my life—and that's saying something. I decided, without much resolve, that I wouldn't see Michael again. I was done. I could only take so much blatant rejection.

We both caught our separate flights back to Birmingham. I would have stayed in New York to pout and stew, but I had meetings. And the next week, he called, as usual. "Are you free tomorrow night?"

And despite my best efforts, despite the no that tried to form itself on my lips, I said yes.

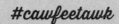

#cawfeetawk

Expectations can really derail people. I tend to jump ahead and figure out exactly what I think is going to happen, but when you let things unfold in their own time without trying to control them, they might just happen in a way that is much better and more powerful than you ever could have orchestrated yourself.

– *Chapter 5* –

DADDY ISSUES

*A*t this point you are probably wondering why I agreed to keep seeing Michael. I was wondering, too. I had said I was done. I had so much more going on in my life. I had plenty of other prospects—men who would be perfectly willing to have sex *on the first date, or even the fifth*, if that's what I wanted. But for some reason, no matter how many times my head said I was done, my heart protested. When I was really honest with myself, I realized that nobody had ever made me feel as much or as strongly as Michael did. Even without sex . . . heck, even without *kissing* . . . I felt him so strongly that I couldn't give him up. If I did, I would only be punishing myself. I wanted to be with him. I sat down one day to think about it logically:

1. He'd shown me nothing but respect.
2. He made me want to be a better person, and I liked that feeling.
3. Up until Michael, I had controlled everything in my life. When you control so much about your own life and someone comes into your world and starts leading

the way and you find yourself giving up the reins, that
means something.

4. I didn't want it all to be in vain. I couldn't just write it
off because he didn't kiss me soon enough, or have sex
according to my schedule.

5. And finally . . . what if his way worked? What if he
was on to something? What if we actually ended up
together because we didn't do all the things that I had
already proven to myself didn't work?

So yes, I went out with him again. I decided it was worth it. I
had to explore this feeling because I hadn't really felt emotionally engaged since my father died.

My father was our rock. A laid-back pot-smoking hippie
type, he was the perfect foil to my mother's histrionics. He was
calm, quiet, contemplative, strong, steady, and he knew what was
important in life. Actually, he was a lot like Michael—if Michael
had been a hippie from Brooklyn. My father was a tall drink of
water and so thin that when he turned sideways, he was like a
sheet of paper. He had long skinny legs and no butt. He had
perfect comedic timing. And everybody loved him. Especially
his children.

We loved the way his silly sense of humor was woven into
his clockwork predictability. He told the same jokes over and
over again. Somehow, they always made us laugh. Whenever
any of us asked him for money, he would take the money out of
his money clip and hand it to us, but as soon as we reached for
it, he would stick his index finger out so we would accidentally
grab his finger. And you know what happens when you pull

somebody's finger. We all thought that was just hilarious. And it was. It still is. Try it sometime.

To be honest, I grew up in a house full of people who farted. Farts in my house were very funny. When there was nothing else to laugh about, somebody would fart and everybody was happy again. My mother was a farter. My father was a farter. All three of us girls were farters, but when my little brother, David, was born, he really raised the bar. David could fart on command, anytime, anywhere. My father was very proud of that.

He had a great laugh and a soft deep voice and he wore a suit every day and every evening at six o'clock, we were all required to sit down at the table with him and eat dinner. He had a diesel Mercedes, and I still associate the rumbling purr and smell of diesel with my father coming home. It didn't matter what we were doing or where we thought we had to be. It wasn't an option, and nobody was allowed to get up from the table until everybody was done. It was a family priority. He wanted to spend that hour with his children. My father was a constant and steady source of unconscious security for me—the kind of security that you aren't even aware of until it's gone. *My father was like gravity.* We all just took it for granted that he would always be there.

And every single night, he would come home from work and go to the cabinet and take a pack of Virginia Slim Lights out of the carton and put it in his briefcase for the next day. This was a fond memory, too, until I realized that this was what was killing him.

In August 1992, just after my brother turned ten, my father started coughing. It was an annoying, nagging cough like he had something tickling his throat. It wasn't a deep disturbing bronchial smoker's cough or a scary phlegmy pneumonia kind of cough. It sounded like nothing serious, *nonproductive*, as they say, but I remember hearing it all the time. At first, my mother thought he was allergic to the dog, so she gave the dog away. We were so angry with her, but I think it was an offering to God: *If I give away this dog, let it be a dog allergy.* She had all the carpets cleaned to get rid of any residual dog hair, but the cough stayed.

In April 1993, my sister Meredith was getting married, and my mom finally convinced my dad to go to the doctor. The week before my sister's wedding, the doctor called my mother, not my father, and said, "Susan, the reason he's coughing is because he has a tumor in his lung that's pushing on his esophagus and it's annoying him."

"What does that mean?" my mother said. "Annoying. Annoying doesn't sound bad."

"It means he has lung cancer," the doctor said, bluntly.

She didn't tell my father until after the wedding, so he could enjoy himself. After the wedding, she broke the news. I remember I was working at the movie theater when my sister picked me up from work. She was crying.

"Daddy has lung cancer," she said.

"What does that mean?" I asked her. I was sixteen years old.

"It means he's really sick."

To me, sick meant sick. Sick didn't mean dying. I didn't want any further clarification. I was like my mother in that way. *Tell me he's sick, but don't tell me anything worse. I don't want to hear it.*

My mother made it very clear that nobody was allowed to talk about my father dying. We could only talk about what we would do when he got better. Nobody had the opportunity to talk to him about what might happen next. Nobody got to ask him what he might want us to know before he was gone, and nobody got to tell him what they would want him to know before he was gone. We were all in denial; anything else was tacitly forbidden. My mother was devoted to keeping the mood positive and upbeat. Then, when she thought nobody would notice, she would go behind the shed in the backyard to cry. She thought I didn't know what she was doing, but I followed her once, spying just to see where she went when she mysteriously disappeared. That's when I realized that maybe my father was sicker than I thought. Still, I didn't want to think about how sick. I refused to think he might be *that sick*. My father hung the moon and therefore *could not die*. Every time the thought threatened to slide into my conscious mind, I pushed it back down. When you're sixteen and your father is the strongest man you know, even a word like *cancer* can't really scare you because it's your dad. It's going to be fine. There could be no other option.

But of course, there was another option. My father went through chemo, and would lock himself in the bathroom to throw up. I watched him lose his hair. He did radiation and I remember the burns on his skin that he tried to hide. My boyfriend at the time, who had many bad qualities, was really good to my dad. I'll give him that. I remember the day he went into the garage with my dad and shaved my dad's head, then shaved his own head, out of solidarity. My dad got weaker and weaker, skinnier and skinnier. Finally he decided he didn't want to do the treatments anymore. He just wanted to smoke weed and be happy. So that's what he did. He would sit alone and smoke and I would watch him from the other room, but I was too afraid to talk to him alone. Too afraid I might see something or that he might tell me something that would kill the hope I still held in my heart.

October 30 is Mischief Night in New Jersey. It's a regional thing—it is the night before Halloween, and the night that separates the tricks from the treats. Kids go out and play practical jokes on people, egging houses, toilet-papering trees, slathering shaving cream and soap on cars. October 30, 1993, was six months after my dad's diagnosis, and it was also my sister Carolyn's twenty-first birthday. She was going to Atlantic City because she could finally gamble. Her boyfriend was going with her, and a few of her friends. This was a very big deal in New Jersey, a ritual everyone completed when they turned twenty-one. She was beyond excited about it.

Because there was so much going on that night, I ended up alone in the kitchen, eating dinner with my father. There was something in the air. It didn't feel right. We were eating soup, and suddenly I looked up at him as he tried to spoon soup into his mouth. His hand was shaking and the soup was spilling from the spoon and he couldn't seem to get the spoon into his mouth. I was embarrassed. He looked up and caught my eye, and smiled weakly—a smile of apology. For what? For not being able to eat soup in front of me? For being sick? For what was about to happen? I looked down and shook my head, trying to erase the image from my mind. I didn't say anything. I wish I'd said something—I wish I'd told him that I saw, and that it was okay, I didn't mind and I didn't hold it against him. But I couldn't admit any of it because acknowledging any weakness in him felt like opening the door to something dark and dangerous.

I hadn't really seen him like this up close. When you're in a room full of people, you can distract yourself from what you don't want to see, but there it was, that night, right in front of me. It was just him and me and it made me worried and filled up with grief. I really hadn't fully realized how much he had declined until that meal together. After dinner, I went upstairs where Carolyn and her girlfriends were getting ready. My mom was helping them.

"I don't think you should go," I blurted out.

"What?" Carolyn looked at me, immediately suspicious that I was trying to ruin her birthday.

"I was eating dinner with Daddy and he doesn't look good. I don't think you should go."

Carolyn sniffed. "You're trying to make me feel bad 'cause you can't go," she said.

"No I'm not. I don't want to go to stupid Atlantic City. I'm just telling you, something's not right. I think we should all stay here . . ."

My mom interrupted. "Don't worry, Jaime. It'll be fine." She patted my shoulder. I shoved her away and stormed downstairs. My boyfriend showed up at the door. We had been planning to go to a party. I told him I couldn't go but he breezed in and sat down with my dad for a while and they talked. He was never afraid to talk to my dad. He came back over to me and put his arm around me. "We're going," he said. "He's fine. He'll be fine." I turned back around and waved to my father. He smiled mildly and waved a shaky hand. It was the last time I saw him alive.

At the party, I couldn't shake the bad feeling. "My dad's really not doing well," I said to my boyfriend. "I need to start spending more time with him. I had dinner with him tonight and it's really not good."

"Okay," he said. "So do that. Tomorrow. Tonight, you are sleeping over." My boyfriend had already graduated and lived with a roommate in an apartment in Freehold.

"I guess," I said, uneasily. I called my mom and told her I was spending the night with a girlfriend. I'm not sure if she believed it any more than I did, but she agreed, sounding distracted. The next morning, at five thirty, I woke to the sound of my boyfriend's roommate's voice talking on the phone.

"Yeah, she's here, let me get her."

My first thought was: *Oh shit, my mom found out where I am, I'm in trouble.* But it was Meredith on the phone. "You have to come home," she said, her voice shaking.

"Why?" I was already mentally Rolodexing through viable excuses.

"Because Daddy died." She started to sob.

I froze. I couldn't think. And then the thoughts flooded in. *I knew it. I knew it. I had felt it, and nobody would listen to me. I didn't even listen to myself. I should have been there. I should have made them all stay there. I knew it. I felt it.* Now I could feel my whole world crumbling around me.

"What happened?" I said, feeling numb. I couldn't feel the hand that held the phone.

"Mom woke up and she said the room felt still and cold. She looked at Daddy, and she said there was a little bit of blood coming out of his mouth, dribbled onto his pillow. She tried to wake him up and she couldn't. David was at the door yelling, 'Dad! It's Halloween! Get up, Dad! Get up!'"

"Oh God," I said. Hot tears filled my eyes up and ran down my face.

"Then she called the neighbor and said, 'I can't wake Lou up. I have to send David to you.' David was so mad when she wouldn't let him come into the bedroom. Then she made him go next door in his pajamas and he threw a fit. Once he was out of the house, she called nine-one-one. Then she started calling all the relatives. She's been on the phone for an hour."

"And you're just calling me?" I felt panic rising inside me. I was the last to know?

"I just woke up. She didn't even wake me up."

We were both silent for a minute.

"Come home," she said.

When I pulled into the driveway, I saw the ambulance and a crowd of our friends and relatives outside and everybody was sort of crying but trying to hold it together. I don't know that anyone thought he would get better, but gone? Really gone? He wasn't that sick. That had been my reality for months. *He wasn't that sick.* It had only been those last few days that he seemed so bad. I wasn't ready. *I wasn't ready.* Was he? He'd never even gone into the hospital. Later, I found out that a month before he died, when he came home crying and my mother made us all leave the room, he confessed that an animal had darted in front of his car and he had tried to stop but his body wouldn't react. He knew something was going very wrong. It was the first time I had ever seen him cry, but I pushed it out of my mind. My mother had told us he wasn't feeling well and I had accepted it. I had believed that it was something temporary. Later, she told me that they had found out the cancer had spread to his brain, affecting his motor skills, but they didn't think they should tell us. The last month he was alive, he was told he couldn't drive us anywhere anymore. We didn't know why, but somehow we knew not to question. Because it was all going to be okay.

I walked inside like a robot, feeling nothing. The house was in chaos. Together, Meredith and I called Carolyn in Atlantic City. We told her, and she drove straight home. I think she took it the hardest. Her cries were more like a wailing. They were the saddest cries I'd ever heard. We knew they would be. Carolyn kept men at arm's length. My father was the only man she ever truly let in.

I walked upstairs and around the hall toward his room. His cousin stood at the door. "Are you sure you want to see him like this?" I nodded. She stepped aside and I stepped in. The room was dark, cold. I stared at his body, willing him to open his eyes. He looked so peaceful. I got on my knees next to the side of his bed. My insides burned. I felt rage I had never felt before. I had no tools, nothing inside to help me cope. There was no faith, no peace. Only rage. I said good-bye and kissed his head. I noticed the Michael Bolton CD I had bought him for his birthday on his nightstand. I felt sick. The room started to spin. After a few minutes that felt like hours, I stood up and walked out. Like a zombie, making my way through clusters of grown men and women consoling one another, I found my way to the TV room and sat, staring at the wall in disbelief.

I remember watching the coroner wheel him out on a stretcher, his body inside a black bag. I watched them bring him down the steps, a man on each corner. I felt a moment of gratitude that he'd died at home in his own bed, rather than in a hospital, hooked up to machines. He would have hated that.

He was fifty-three years old.

When you're Jewish and someone dies, the family sits shiva

as a ritual of mourning. We covered all the mirrors, and all the chairs were taken out of the house and replaced with cardboard boxes. We all sat on the boxes while people came in to pay their respects for days.

Jersey Jews

Sitting shiva is a practice that symbolizes the mourner being "brought low" following the loss of a loved one. Nobody sends flowers, but they all bring food. It is a ritual meant to compress the mourning period—to get it all out so that everyone can go back to their lives. Sometimes this works. Sometimes it doesn't.

But of course, life was never the same after that. Losing my father changed me. It changed all of us. It robbed us of a certain innocence that I think children deserve to keep for an extended period of time. Certainly longer than seventeen years. Losing your father makes you realize that tomorrow isn't a promise, and when you're seventeen you don't want to think about that. You want to believe there are a million more tomorrows, but suddenly you know there aren't. There might not be any at all.

Before he died, I was a child, and after he died I was something in between child and adult—something angry and hard. I was angry at things I couldn't change. I was angry that my mother was falling apart. I was angry that my sisters were old enough to move out and I had to stay. I was angry that my brother, my poor brother, who had been so full of joy and happiness and energy, was suddenly doomed to live in a house with women who never stopped crying.

I stopped caring about anyone.

And this brings me back to Michael. Michael, who wouldn't kiss me, who was so impossibly calm and collected, who was so much older. I never wanted to be one of those people who lost a father and searched forever for a replacement, and I don't believe Michael was a replacement. But there was something about him that made me feel again. After years of short-term relationships and long-term relationships, loving people the wrong way and never being able to make anything work, after years of leaving people before they disappointed me or loving people I knew would hurt me because I didn't deserve to be happy, Michael made me feel something different. I couldn't explain it. I couldn't apply logic, and I don't even want to know what a shrink would say. But the truth was that I loved him. And so I forgave his snail's-pace courtship. And I stayed.

But not without a plan.

#cawfeetawk

Everyone handles death differently, but the one thing we all have in common when we lose someone we love with everything we've got is that we are forever changed. That change can feel painful, involving suffering and mourning and even guilt, but it can also be transformative, drawing us closer to things we may not have fully realized were the most important in life, such as family, friends, and faith.

Chapter 6

AND THEN HE KISSED ME

The next time I went out with Michael, I decided I would try a bluff. We were on a date at a Mexican restaurant, having drinks. As soon as the server put my margarita in front of me, I took a big swig for courage and laid it on the line. I said, "Listen, Michael. I don't want to do this anymore. I think we should pay the tab, go back to your house, have sex, and then stop dating. I really don't want to be the girl you take out for dinner once a week for the rest of my life. But I *would* really like to get laid. No strings. No promises. Let's just do it, and then we can both move on with our separate lives."

He laughed. "No."

"What do you mean, no?"

"I mean no."

I stared at him. "You can't just say no."

"Of course I can." He took a calm sip of his beer.

"Well, then, I don't want to see you anymore," I said, a note of hysteria in my voice.

"Yes you do," he said.

"No! I don't!" I insisted. "This is boring to me. Boring. I'm bored with this . . . this . . . whatever this is!"

Just then, the waitress came up to the table. She took our orders, and Michael continued on with our previous conversation, like I'd never said anything at all. Michael: 1. Jaime's bluff: 0.

Life went on like this. We would go out once a week. Occasionally, I would try to break up with him, he would ignore me, I would realize I didn't really want to break up with him, and the next week I'd find myself out to dinner with him again.

In the eighth month, something changed. One week, when he called me to ask me if I was free and I said I was, instead of telling me where we were going and confirming that we would meet there, he asked me to meet him at his house. I pulled into the driveway, matching bra and panties on, sure that I was what was on the menu. To my dismay, he was standing in the driveway, keys in hand. He opened my door. "Come on, jump in my car, I'll drive."

And this is how it continued. I would arrive, and he would already be outside, waiting. We would get into his car and go on the date in the same vehicle. I would look longingly at the exterior of his home and imagine what it might look like inside. A quintessential bachelor's pad? All dark wood and expensive leather? Full of golf trophies or mounted animal heads? Stacks of porn? I had no idea and he never, ever invited me in. Still, somehow, it felt like progress. After the date, he would pull up behind my car, come around to the passenger side, open the door for me, and walk me to my car. I would thank him for dinner, he would open my car door for me, and I would get in and drive home. But lip contact? Body contact? A simple hug? A polite *Do you want to come in for a drink?* None of it.

In the ninth month, there was another subtle change. He began offering to pick me up. Sometimes I accepted. But more often, I would say no, because I really didn't know what was happening and I didn't want him controlling everything. And somehow, to me, meeting at his house had more promise than being picked up at my house. Because I knew if I invited him in for a drink, he would decline. I had the instinct that the closer I was to his front door, the better. One night, when he walked me to my car, I opened the door and I was standing between the door and the car and out of nowhere, with no warning, he leaned in and kissed me for the first time.

Whoa, buddy.

It was awkward. It was weird. I had no mental preparation for it, not even a chance to check my hair or lick my lips or make sure I didn't have anything between my teeth. And the kiss itself . . . ugh. It was nothing I had hoped and dreamed it would be. Have you ever seen people trying to do a three-legged race and fighting each other and stumbling all over the place instead of working together in sync and sailing to the finish line? The awkward stumblers are funny, right? This was just like that.

Except it wasn't funny. It was awful. I mean awful. We both tried to turn our heads the same way. We bumped teeth. It was dry and clumsy and I was like, *Uh, what is he doing? Don't I get any warning?* And he was probably like, *Uh, what is she doing? I thought she wanted this.* Where was Shonda Rhimes when you needed her? There was no "moment," no dreamy tenderness, no eye contact that said without words, *Yes, we both want it, let's kiss.* Was he trying to do me a favor? Was I expecting too much? I was so confused and embarrassed that I just got into my car and drove away without saying a word. I couldn't even look him in the eye. I couldn't believe I'd waited nine months for *that*. It was just gross and bad. And gross.

As soon as I got home, I called my sister Meredith. "You are going to fucking die," I said.

"What, what?" she said.

"He finally kissed me!"

"Oh my God, tell me everything," she said. "Every detail. Leave nothing out."

"There is nothing to tell," I said. "Except that it was *awful*." I could hear my Jersey accent coming out in full force, as if trying to remind me how much I did not belong in Alabama with its stiff, overly proper, bad-kissing men. "It. Was. AWWWWW-ful."

"What? How? Why? No, no, no, that can't be," she said. "He's sexy."

"He's fooled us all!" I yelled. "It was all a lie! Nobody who kisses like that can possibly be sexy," I went on. "We couldn't get on the same page. Everyone was going at a different speed, he expected to lead, I had no interest in letting him lead, face parts were smacking against face parts. I can't even think about it, it was just humiliating." Just then, a terrible thought struck me. "Is it me? Is this the kind of kiss *I* inspire? Oh God!"

"Jaime. Reality check. It's obviously not you. You are a sensual gorgeous woman."

"Okay. Thank you. But then . . . what the hell was it? What have I been doing for nine months? This is my big payoff?"

"Maybe it was just a bad first try. I'm sure he can do better. Maybe he was nervous."

"It could improve a hundred percent and still be terrible. That's how terrible it was. I can't even begin to see how anybody could improve sufficiently from whatever that was."

"What are you going to do?" she said.

"I don't know," I said. "I *really* like him but I don't see how this can work. If a guy can't kiss well, how can he be *the guy*? This kiss is telling. The kiss is the first big sign that this can't work."

Meredith sighed. "I thought you had chemistry."

"Me, too," I said, miserably.

But some sane part of me told the drama queen in me to chill out and let him—let *us*—have another chance. On our next date, he kissed me again, and it was better. Still not good, but better. I was still deeply disappointed, but I also wondered if Meredith was right. Underneath that calm, cool, collected southern demeanor, maybe he was actually horribly nervous and it was affecting his performance. How would he kiss if he was 100 percent comfortable and sure of me? Then again, a kiss is a kiss and chemistry is chemistry. And obviously we did not kiss well together at all.

And then, it happened. *It*. That's right. Exactly what you are thinking. Ten months in, on the third date after the first kiss. It all happened at once. From zero to sixty. From dud to dude. From snail's pace to the Jersey speed limit. Well, after a little bit of swerving.

#cawfeetawk

Kissing is a form of communication and it takes some people lon-ger than others to open up. Just like conversation, sometimes you have to show your partner how you want to receive their message—hopefully without a wrong slip of the tongue!

Chapter 7

TAMPONS, HUMILIATION, AND THE ULTIMATE PRIZE

It started out like any other date. We went out to dinner, we had a great night, we were in sync, we were laughing, it was lighthearted and fun, and when we got back to his house and he pulled up behind my car, he got out, opened my door, and . . . didn't walk me to my car. Instead, without any warning signs or hints or clues (I was beginning to recognize that Michael doesn't do clues), he began walking toward the side door of his house.

"Where are you going?" I said.

"Inside," he said. "Would you like to have a drink?"

I stared at him. "Really?"

"Sure, why not?" he said, as if it was the most natural thing in the world, as if it was something he asked me after every date. As if he expected that I would just *follow him in there, without an invitation.*

I was immediately suspicious. I thought, *Progress, yes. But what does this mean? Is this our new routine for the next six months? We go inside, have a drink, go back outside, kiss awkwardly, and I drive home? I can hardly wait.* But I followed him in. Just. In. Case.

He made us drinks. I slid up onto the low kitchen counter to sit, and he was talking, and we were laughing, and he walked over to me while I was sitting on the counter with my drink, and he kissed me. Like, really kissed me. *Holy shit, where did that come from?* It was a real kiss. A passionate, thrill-inducing, totally connected kiss. It was a butterflies-in-your-vagina kiss. He looked at me and I think I truly saw him for the first time. His guard was down. His walls had crumbled. He was showing me the real Michael Sullivan, and he was a little boy, an awkward teenager, a grown man who didn't completely know what he was doing in that moment, but whose blue eyes simmered with desire and raw wanting. I could see right into him. I could see that he was comfortable being the man out in the world, but not so comfortable baring his soul like this, and that he had only decided to do this because I was worth it. I was worth the wait, and I was the source of his desire. Hallelujah!

I threw my arms around his neck and kissed him right back with everything I had. He pulled back and looked me right in the eye. Although his voice stuttered just a little, he said the words I'd waited almost ten months to hear. He said: "D-do you want to stay?"

I wanted to say, *Aw, buddy, it's okay, you're so cute, but you don't have to be so nervous. I'm a sure thing!* I wanted to say, *My God, are we a pair of fucked-up souls right now? But let's dive in anyway and figure it out!* And I wanted to say, *Michael Sullivan, I love you with my entire heart and soul and I never want to be without you!* But I didn't say any of those things. I just grinned and nodded. And then I thought, *Shit, if I had known this was going to happen, I would have worn cuter underwear.*

He took my hand and helped me off the counter. He walked me up the steps to the bedroom. He was gentle, ironically, considering what I knew we were about to do. He could have picked me up and carried me upstairs, or thrown me against a wall, for that matter. I would have been fine with that. But this was good, too. *We'll do it his way*, I thought, not for the first time, and not for the last.

He brought me into the bedroom, sat me down on the bed, and turned toward the bathroom. "I'll be back in a minute," he said.

Moving like lightning, I ripped off all my clothes, turned off the light, turned on the TV with no volume so there was a more flattering glow that would disguise my back fat, and assumed the Greek goddess position. I was on my side. I stuck out my collarbones, sucked in my stomach, and arranged my boobs so one wasn't falling into the other one. Perfect. And . . . hold!

Two minutes passed. Five minutes. Now my stomach muscles were cramping and I was scared I was going to have to fart. My mouth was getting dry. Ten minutes passed. I was losing interest in looking skinny. After fifteen, I was lying on my back counting cracks in the ceiling. By twenty, I was going through the drawers in his bedside table. Don't judge. The guy asks me to come to his room and then goes off to take a dump? He deserves to have his stuff searched.

Eventually, I end up sitting naked, Indian-style, poking holes in expired condoms. I couldn't believe how many expired condoms he had in that bedside table. Do you know how old condoms have to be to expire? They're like canned goods. I had them spread all over the bed. How long had these been in his drawer? How long had it been since he'd had a woman in his bedroom? *How many of these did he think we were going to need?* None, that's how many, because they were expired and he had clearly died on the pot.

Finally he came out of the bathroom, startling me. I looked up from my condom-poking project and stared. There he was, in his boxer shorts . . . with a tampon stuck up each nostril.

"What the hell?" I said.

"I'm so sorry," he said, his voice plugged up due to the tampons and the humiliation. "I'm having the worst nosebleed I've ever had in my life." I looked at him. He looked at the expired condoms all over the bed. I realized it was the first time I'd ever seen his nipples. Not that there was anything wrong with his nipples. They were perfectly normal nipples, but you forget that people have nipples until you see them for the first time, and then you are preoccupied: *Oh. Nipples. He has them. There they are.*

Then I snapped out of it. He was in distress. And bleeding. "Oh my God, let me see," I said. I jumped off the bed, still totally naked, and played nurse. We took the tampons out of his nose, which, by the way, is totally *not sexy*, in case anyone is thinking of using this for future seductions. I turned the light on. I grabbed my shirt and put it on. Because who wants to be naked like that in front of somebody for the first time, in the harsh light, while handling bloody tampons?

"Why do you even have tampons in your house?" I had to ask.

"I get nosebleeds," he said. "Bad ones. So I keep these around. They work better than anything else I've tried."

"Resourceful," I said.

"I'm fine, it's fine," he said, looking completely miserable.

"No it's not, you're really bleeding," I said.

"I ruined it," he said.

I couldn't help smiling. "You didn't ruin it," I said. "It's not your fault."

We looked at each other. "I was waiting there like a Greek goddess and you took forever," I said, just so he would know that I had put some effort into the whole thing.

"I would have liked to see that," he said, tilting his head down.

"I was looking really hot for a couple of minutes there," I said.

"Can we start over and pretend this never happened?" he said. "I think the bleeding has stopped." He lifted his head back up. I nodded.

I turned off the lights. He went back in the bathroom. I assumed the position. He came out and pretended like it was the first time he'd seen me naked. He really looked, and I could see it in his eyes. He wanted me. *Thank God.*

And then I thought . . . *panicked* might be a more exact word: *I'm about to have sex with someone I really like. This is significant. This matters.*

Part of me couldn't believe this was finally, actually happening, and another part of me was terrified. After waiting this long, what was this going to mean? Were the rules different now? I was used to having sex with people before I was completely sure I really liked them, so the stakes had never been so high. *I think I might really love this person . . . and . . . and . . . oh my God . . . I've never seen his penis!*

The penis.

Uh-oh. Suddenly, the thought consumed me. His penis! It was an unknown quantity! I'd never even felt it. You know how, when you make out with a guy, you can usually tell what he's working with because you feel it against your leg? I had zero information. Nada. There were no frisky hand jobs, no one-too-many-martini blowies, nothing. Michael had never allowed the opportunity. And I thought, *Oh my God, how awkward is this going to be if he gets in bed and he's got a gherkin? What if he's hung like a cheese doodle? How did I get this far without knowing for sure? Is this the secret strategy of those who aren't well endowed? Do they get you to fall in love with them first, and hope size doesn't matter? How is this going to work? What do you do when that happens? Do you just have really-small-penis sex for the rest of your life? Do you have to tell yourself that it isn't about the size, it's about what you do with it?*

I was terrified. I felt shallow and silly and I was having an anxiety attack. Thoughts of how I could get out of the relationship without him knowing it was because of his very small penis flooded my brain. As he kissed me, I was thinking, *My first move should be to get out of the house. I could say I had to let the dog out. Oh no, I'm so sorry, Michael! I forgot to let the dog out! I can't continue having the sex, because of the dog!*

And then . . . *Wait a minute. I think I feel something on my leg.* In my sexiest voice, I whispered, "Are you gonna keep those boxers on all night?" He got all shy, blushing the way he does, and took them off.

Jackpot.

It was beautiful. It was just what I wanted. I couldn't believe how well it all worked. That night erased the memory of the horrible first kiss, replacing it with much better, shall we say bigger, memories. It was great sex. Vanilla sex, to be sure—nothing kinky, nothing crazy, no Kama Sutra positions, no falling off the bed or doing it upside down and backward, but it was the very best vanilla sex I'd ever had. Top-shelf Tahitian vanilla sex. I was in love and it was awesome.

Afterward, not knowing what to expect, I got off the bed and started to get dressed. "What are you doing?" he asked.

"Early morning. It's late."

He sat up. "You can't leave." There was something about the way he said it that I knew he meant it. I had to stay. Got it. This was clearly a thing for him. It was the way he differentiated casual sex from non-casual sex. I had to be there in the morning to make it official. We had done it, and that changed things. Was it a southern thing, or just a Michael thing? I didn't know, and in the afterglow I didn't really care.

"All right then." I slipped back out of my jeans, climbed back into bed, curled into him, and fell deeply, soundly, gloriously asleep.

The next morning, he brought me coffee in bed (he still does that, eleven years later, and it's one of the things I love best about him). We sat there together drinking coffee and reading the newspaper.

I took a sip of my coffee and looked at him. He had his reading glasses on and the sports page open. "Oh my God," I said. "This is going to be my life now, isn't it?" I said. "I'm going to date the old man who reads the newspaper in bed! I am dating my dad. I'm officially dating my dad!"

He shook his head, in that way he does, as if to say, *Only you, babe.*

Later that morning, I kissed him good-bye and went to work. I felt like I'd been deflowered. I felt like a woman. It was weird. And wonderful.

And he was different from that moment on, too. I can't quite put my finger on it, but he was different. Once we had sex, it was like something clicked in his mind and the relationship parameters changed. For one thing, he had never come to visit me at my office. He'd never even seen my office. The day after we had sex, he called me.

"I'm at the Starbucks near your office, would you like something?"

I said yes, just to see if he would actually show up. He did. I went outside to meet him in the parking lot and I said, "Do you realize this is the first time you've ever driven to my office?"

"Oh, is it?" He can be so coy, but I sensed that he felt newly entitled to go where I was, to be where I worked, to be an integral part of my life.

The girls in the office of the magazine were watching out the window. When I came back in, they all wanted to know why he was there. They knew he never came to the office. I had told them all about him.

"We finally did it," I said, smugly.

"You did it?!" Every one of them was wide-eyed.

"Yeah we did."

It's funny because that's all they needed to know.

Southern girls don't ask you the details. If that had been an office full of my Jersey girls, they'd have been like, *Oh my gawd, tell me everything, does he have a big dick?* I was assuming and sort of hoping they would so I could tell them how nice it was, but nobody asked. Freaking southern chicks, they suck all the joy out of your dirty stories.

Michael wasn't the only changed one. There was a shift in how we moved together, how we were together, how we kissed. We finally got in sync, and that is what it was really all about. There was a familiarity between us that could never have been there had we not done it his way. When you date all full of lust and impulse, you can't possibly build that kind of foundation. When you do it in the beginning, it can't possibly have as much meaning. The whole next day, all I could think of was, "What took you so long?" The thought buzzed happily through my mind like a message on a marquee. But I was beginning to understand the answer.

#cawfeetawk

As good as it can feel to move zero to sixty, life can't sustain that. I highly recommend waiting at least four to six months before sharing intimate and vulnerable parts of yourself or growing attached to someone, whether romantic partner or friend. It takes at least this long for a person's true intentions to surface.

Chapter 8

ROSE-COLORED GLASSES

I was in heaven . . . for a while. Michael and I had sealed the deal in June, and things were definitely different after that. But not as different as I thought they would be. After all the energy and focus I had put into the relationship, after how long I had waited, how patient I had been, how loving, and frankly, how creative and wifely I had tried to seem during our ensuing sexual encounters, things seemed to hover in place. They call it "ring fucking." Crude, I know, but honestly, that's what I was doing—being extra attentive and especially sexy and wearing lingerie and handing out blow jobs like they were candy as incentive for him to propose to me. But I wasn't getting the ring. We never even discussed marriage. And why? Wasn't that what this had all been about? Sure, the energy had changed. We were more physically and emotionally connected. But how many years was *this* going to go on before I got to take my rightful place as Mrs. Michael Sullivan?

Then, Las Vegas happened.

I had to go to Vegas for the weekend, to cover the JCK LUXURY show—the jewelry industry's biggest trade show of the year—for the Birmingham-based magazine I was working for. In addition to handling the magazine's marketing, I often wrote travel and luxury articles for them. Normally I would have considered Vegas a time to cut loose and maybe meet someone interesting, but I was completely blissed out about Michael, and so focused on my marital goals that this trip felt merely like work. I was going to Vegas with Abi, one of my good friends from Los Angeles. We would meet, share a hotel room, get our work done, and have some girl-time, gambling and drinking champagne. When Michael dropped me off at the airport, I said good-bye, kissed him passionately, and went in to find my gate. As I flew from Birmingham, I closed my eyes and thought about Michael in the most romantic way. I was smitten, and loving it. I landed, met Abi, and in the cab to our hotel I got the text that nearly changed my life forever:

Hey, friend. Hope you're safe in Vegas. Have a good time and enjoy yourself. I don't want you to see this relationship through rose-colored glasses.

What the fuck?

I read it again and again and I showed it to Abi. I had just been telling her all about Michael, and how sure I was that he must be on the verge of proposing.

She read it and looked up at me.

"Rose-colored glasses? What is he, one of the Golden Girls?"

"I know, right? And why is he calling me *friend*?"

"The F-word. What the fuck?" said Abi.

"Exactly."

We both stared at my phone for a minute. Abi looked at me. "What does he mean by *enjoy yourself*? Is he giving you some kind of free pass?"

My heart sank. I got angry, then scared. I had always been

afraid of being left, of letting my heart go out to somebody, of being vulnerable, and ultimately being left behind with no warning. All my fears seemed to be coming to pass. *Friend? Enjoy yourself*? None of it made any sense when I thought about the progression of my relationship with Michael—and yet, on the other hand, maybe it did. Maybe he had waited ten months to have sex with me because he wasn't really that interested. Maybe he finally gave in because he knew how much I wanted it. Maybe it was pity sex. It hadn't *seemed* like pity sex. Not for a second. But I had always played it cool, like I didn't care that much, and now that I was showing how much I cared, was he throwing it back in my face? Was he telling me he wanted the old, carefree Jaime who couldn't commit? Was that safer for him? Or was this some kind of test?

I was so confused and overwhelmed that I didn't know what to do. But I had work to get done. I couldn't be depressed. I couldn't be scared. I was a professional woman in Vegas and my success or failure would directly impact the magazine and possibly my career path. So I opted for angry. I would be pissed. I would do exactly what he suggested. He was just a "friend," after all. I would *not* see the relationship through rose-colored glasses. I would see it for exactly what it was: a big fat question mark. And I *would* enjoy myself, fully. If that's what Michael wanted, that's what Michael would get.

"Fuck it," I said to Abi. "I'm going to have fun. Forget him. If he's still on the fence after all this time, I am not going to waste one more second mooning over him."

"Amen, sis-tah!" she said, and high-fived me. "Let's get changed and hit the bar."

"I would like nothing more," I said. "I have to meet one client, and then I'll meet you at the casino."

I put my BlackBerry in my purse. I would entertain no further communication from Michael Sullivan while I was busy working and partying in Vegas. I didn't have the life energy to waste on games. I had a presentation to do.

My most important client was first on my list. I had agreed to a few pitch meetings to sell advertising to some of the big luxury brands, and this particular Swiss watch company was a major client with a major budget. I had to get this right. After that, I could find Abi, have a drink, do some gambling, and dance the night away.

Most appointments that I had set for the week were down on the trade show floor, but this particular brand was so elite that they had their own suite with high-level security. Usually I met with the marketing team, but rumor had it that the president of the brand was very hands-on and would sit in on the meeting. It was a little intimidating, but I imagined he would be some short burly man, probably balding and sweaty. He was probably old, and he was Swiss, which is pretty much the same as German, right? And he probably wouldn't really be listening to me anyway—he would delegate ad decisions to others. So I shook it off.

I buzzed up to the hotel room, changed into a straight black business skirt and jacket, put on my business-lady heels, brushed my hair, grabbed my briefcase, and walked up to the suite. As soon as I found the number, I paused. The door was gilded and I could hear the harsh sound of Swiss-German voices from behind it. I took a deep breath and knocked. A tall blond woman with her hair in a tight, neat bun answered. I smiled broadly and breezed in past her, all confidence and business. I looked around—the suite was very posh and everyone looked impossibly polished and very tall and blond and Swiss. Now, I'm pretty tall myself, but suddenly I felt short and dumpy and . . . very Jersey, in a bad way.

"He will be with you shortly," the woman said coolly in a heavy accent, and left me alone. *He?* The company president? It wasn't clear, so I sat. Ten minutes passed. Fifteen. Then thirty friggin' minutes passed. I was already angry at Michael, and now I was getting angry at *everything*. Why was I sitting here in this fancy suite, doing nothing, surrounded by oblivious Swiss people speaking a language I couldn't understand? I could be downstairs gambling and partying with Abi, but *no*. No one came to check on me. No one even offered me a cup of coffee or a glass of water. They all just milled about, murmuring in what was gibberish to me. It was like I was invisible.

Finally, I had had enough. I stood up, ready to walk right out of there, no longer caring whether I scored the account. Then I heard a voice. It was a resonant voice, a Swiss-German voice, a *sexy voice*. Suddenly I felt nervous. I had been ready to storm out the door, but now I hesitated. Something about his tone made my whole body tingle. What was happening? Who was it? He came out of a door, turned toward me, and began striding down the hall. My jaw actually dropped.

He was not round or short or sweaty. He was gorgeous. *Gor-geous.* Our eyes locked.

You know how they say dolphins communicate with each other by sending sonic waves through the water? This was like that—I felt like I'd been hit by a dolphin sonic boom. Holy shit. He turned to his entourage and spoke in a stern and intimidating voice to them, in Swiss-German, and suddenly they were all flocking around me: "Do you want some coffee? Do you want some water? Here, have some pineapple!"

Pineapple?

And wait, I thought. *You motherfuckers speak English?* No one had said word one to me for half an hour, and now suddenly ten people are trying to get me to eat a pineapple?

Then he came up to me with his magnificent accent with his stunning blue-gray eyes and broad shoulders and cheekbones looking all sexy-*Die-Hard*-villain-y. And he spoke.

"So sorry to keep you waiting." He extended his strong, tanned, masculine hand. "I'm Thomas."

Yes you are. You are Thomas all day long and twice on Sundays.

"Well . . ." I said, trying to sound indignant. "I'm Jaime."

"You have something to show me, yes? I'm all ears," he said, and he smiled. A German accent had *never* sounded so sexy. And that smile! I was completely disarmed.

Thomas sat and his entire entourage sat, too, as if on cue. They all stared at me expectantly. I felt completely unprepared. Thirty minutes in an empty room and suddenly it was like opening night on Broadway. Thomas sat in front on the couch and gazed at me with those steely blue-gray eyes. His lashes were blond. *Don't get distracted!* I took out my laptop. I handed out a few copies of the magazine. I handed him one with earmarked pages so he could see some of the ads. I cleared my throat. I started my presentation, just the way I always did it. All seemed to be going well.

Then five minutes into my spiel, his phone rang. He got

up and walked out of the room, right in the middle of my sentence. Not even an *Excuse me*.

I paused. Was I supposed to wait for him? Was this some kind of joke? I was embarrassed and insulted. How dare he come in looking all hot and interested, and then walk out on me so rudely! *I don't care how hot you are, dude. If you're walking out on me midsentence, you can blow me. I'm done.* I'd already wasted forty-five minutes of good gambling time. I stopped talking immediately. I collected my magazines, shut my laptop, put everything in my briefcase, and without another word I grabbed my purse and walked right out the door. Everyone just stared at me but no one tried to stop me. Once I was safely down the hall, I dug my phone out of my purse and called Abi.

"That motherfucker."

"What happened?"

"He was so rude, he kept me waiting for half an hour, then he had the nerve, five minutes into my presentation, to answer his phone and walk out of the room."

"What a dickhead. Come on, let's go gamble."

"I'm getting in the elevator right now, I'll see you in a minute."

I got in the elevator, pressed L, and rode down to the lobby. I stepped onto the casino floor feeling flustered and frustrated. I scanned the floor for Abi when my phone rang. It was a long weird number, +44, a 0, two 1s . . . what the hell was this?

"Hello?"

"Is this Jaime?" I knew that voice.

"It is."

"You left. You didn't even say good-bye."

"I don't say good-bye to people who are rude to me, who

keep me waiting thirty minutes and then walk right out on me when I'm giving my presentation." I was furious. Even more furious now, saying it to him out loud. It sounded just and righteous and I had every reason to be pissed. "Besides, how do I say good-bye to somebody who isn't even in the room?"

"That was a very important business call that I had to take."

"Then you look at me and you say, *Excuse me, could you give me a minute? This is important.* That's what a polite person would do. But instead, you left me standing up there like an asshole." Oh my God, was I giving etiquette lessons to the president of the company?

"You're not an asshole," he said.

"*I* know that, but do you know that? Because you left me standing there like an asshole."

"I want to see you. Come back," he said. His calm steady voice infuriated me even more. Especially because it was so sexy.

"Yeah, right. Not interested but nice meeting you, *sir*, and have a good show."

Just as I was about to hang up, he said, "Jaime."

"*What?*"

"You left your briefcase up here."

Shit. Seriously? This was going to blow my whole dramatic kiss-off scene.

"No I didn't . . . did I?" I realized I wasn't holding it. I looked around. It wasn't here. I remembered: I'd put everything back into it, snapped the lid, and stormed out without it. Business fail!

"I'm holding it in my hand," he stated matter-of-factly.

Are you fucking kidding me?

"Fine. I'll be right there. But only for a second!" As if my abbreviated presence would be some kind of punishment for this incredibly rich and powerful Swiss businessman. Feeling both blameless and ridiculous, I marched back up to the suite and knocked on the door. This time, he opened the door himself. His suit jacket was off. His top button was unbuttoned. He had a drink in his hand, and everybody else was gone. It was probably twelve minutes since I'd walked out. In twelve minutes, he had dismissed the whole crew and started the party?

"I'd like to apologize," he said. God, that was a sultry voice for a man. "And I'd still like to hear your presentation."

"I'm done for the day. You don't get to hear my presentation," I said. "Now please, give me my briefcase."

He smiled luxuriantly and leaned against the door frame. "Tell me what you know about Switzerland."

"Oh my God. Nothing. Snow. Chocolate. Banks. Cheese . . . Neutral. Now can I have my briefcase?" I tried to look irritated, but I could feel him sucking me in.

"Yes, we don't get involved in any wars. We are a peaceful people."

"Okay. Great. This conversation is riveting. I'm having a real blast. But my girlfriend is waiting for me downstairs," I said. "I really need to go."

"What do I need to do to hold your attention?" he said.

My first thought? *Take off your pants.* Instead, I said, "Look, I don't know what kind of David Blaine/Jedi mind trick you're trying to do here right now." He was delish but I was a rational, grown woman with a boyfriend—at least, I *thought* I had a boyfriend. I could not handle this strange random encounter. "I just wanna go gamble and party and have a good time."

"Then let's go," he said.

"You can't go. Don't you have . . . meetings or whatever?"

He looked around, amused, at the empty room. "I'm the president," he said. "I can do what I want."

God, that was sexy. "Look," I said, deciding I'd better just lay it on the line. "I understand you are powerful. Apparently you can banish thirty Swiss people to some random closet on a whim. You can leave your duties for the whole day. I get it. You're Zeus. But my friend and I are going to go hang out, and I'll see you when I see you." I spotted my briefcase. I pushed past him, my body brushing his, and I swear, I would guess it was what a wet dream felt like. I stumbled, regained myself, picked it up, turned around, and walked out. Even though my back was to him, he didn't take his eyes off me. I could feel his gaze and it was all I could do to stay upright. I was a paragon of self-control! I went back to the elevator, went downstairs, and found Abi.

"Where were you?" she said. I told her everything that had happened. "Ew. Creepy stalker dude. That's weird," she said. "He probably did something to make you leave your briefcase."

"Obviously," I said. "Some Swiss . . . hypnotism technique or something." I didn't mention how incredibly hot he was.

Abi and I went to a dinner at a restaurant that I was reviewing, we ate, we drank, and we had the best time. Just as we were heading toward a club to go dancing, my phone rang. I looked at the number.

"Oh my God. It's Mr. Forty-Four," I said.

"Answer it!" Abi said, grabbing my arm. "I want to hear that freak!"

Since this was in my BlackBerry days, there was no speakerphone. I just turned the volume way up using the little side roller.

"Hello?"

"Where are you?" he said. Abi and I rolled our eyes at each other.

"Where are *you*?" I said, trying to be cute.

"I asked you first."

"What are we, twelve? We just left dinner and we're going to get a drink."

"Where?"

"Wherever," I said.

"Have a drink with me," he said. Abi made a wild *yes* motion.

"Where are you?" I said.

"Behind you."

Abi and I turned around and there he was, standing with some other businessmen, right behind us, in all their Swiss glory. Like the envoy for some perfect Stepford businessman convention. And there *he* was, in what was quite possibly the most gorgeous suit I had ever seen.

"Oh. My. God," Abi whispered. "You didn't tell me they were all so . . ."

I elbowed her. "Shhh!"

She nodded slowly.

"If we go with them, all bets are off," I whispered out of the side of my mouth.

She nodded in agreement. "Michael?"

I felt a twinge of guilt and sorrow but I pushed it down. "Michael who?"

She smiled. "That's my Jaime!"

"Then it's on like Donkey Kong," I said. And I put on my biggest, most radiant smile.

They swept us into an exclusive private room in a gorgeous lounge and we all had a drink. And then another one. We talked and laughed and every one of those guys was clever and handsome and funny and interesting, and they all had the same sexy accent.

We went to a club and danced, and he was just . . . just awesome. The chemistry between us was off-the-charts. He held my hand. He was attentive and sweet, funny and clever, and obviously extremely attracted to me. I couldn't ignore how good it felt to be openly pursued. I had missed that feeling. Abi was having the time of her life, too, getting a lot of attention from two of the other gorgeous men who seemed to be competing for her. At some point during the night, somebody suggested running off to get married and figuring out the rest later.

"You should do it!" Abi said.

"Yeah, right," I said. We were all drunk but by this point, I felt like I had known Thomas my whole life. He put his arm around me companionably and I snuggled into him, trying not to think about Michael. Thomas felt right and good. And I strongly suspected he would *not* wait nine months to kiss me or ten months to sweep me off my feet and carry me into the bedroom. Had I accidentally found my Prince Charming? I never was one to believe in that sort of thing, but Thomas really did seem right out of a fairy tale. A gorgeous blond well-muscled Swiss fairy tale. At three o'clock in the morning, as we sat cuddling on a red velvet banquette in a corner of the hotel, exhausted but not wanting the night to end, I looked up at him and whispered, "Where did you come from?"

He smiled. "Switzerland," he said, and kissed me on the forehead.

He walked me to my hotel room while the two men who had been Abi's shadow all night walked behind us, one on either side of her. They were laughing and talking, but Thomas and I were quiet, suddenly mutually aware (or so it seemed to me) that our connection could possibly be significant, if we allowed it to be. He said good night, and he didn't kiss me. In this case, I knew exactly why. It would have meant too much. I don't remember what I said next. *I'll see you tomorrow?* I don't know. It was very late, and he had to be up at the show by eight AM. Abi and I closed the door, tore off our dresses, climbed into our beds with all our makeup on, and immediately passed out without any discussion.

I woke up a few hours later, at six thirty AM, and I lay in bed for a while, thinking about it all. Thomas. Michael. Thomas. Michael. When I thought of Thomas, I got tingly. When I thought of Michael, I felt sad. I really didn't know what to make of it. But here I was, *not* seeing the relationship through rose-colored glasses. Some part of me knew I was turning away from what was difficult and real and meaningful, and turning toward a fantasy, but the fantasy was so damn beautiful. I wanted to live in that fantasy just a little longer.

I jumped out of bed and turned on my computer while Abi snoozed soundly in the next bed. I went online to try to compose a message in German. I figured out how to say "Thank you for last night" and texted it to him because I knew he would already be up.

I stared at the BlackBerry screen. Nothing.

Finally he texted back, *I can't believe you took the time to write me a message in German. It wasn't Swiss German, but it was wonderful.*

I'm still working out what Swiss German is, I answered. *You'll have to spend some more time explaining it to me.*

I wouldn't miss that opportunity, he wrote back.

I was in meetings all day, but Thomas never left my mind. That night was supposed to be my last night in Vegas. We all went out for dinner—Thomas and I, and Abi and her admirers. After dinner, Thomas took my hand. "You're not leaving tomorrow," he said.

"Yes I am," I said. "My publisher will fire me if I don't get back to work."

"Just stay one more day. What if I buy a full-page ad in your magazine?" he said.

"You're going to spend fifteen thousand dollars on an ad in my magazine just so I'll stay another day?" I said.

"Call your publisher."

It was ten PM in Birmingham, but I called her at home. I informed her that our very important client wanted to speak with her, and put Thomas on the line.

"Hello. Sorry to bother you so late, I'll be forthright. If I buy a full-page ad in your magazine and change her ticket, can Jaime stay one more night?"

She laughed. "If you buy a full-page ad in our magazine, Jaime can do whatever she wants."

Thomas had his assistant call the airline. He paid to change my flight, and Abi's, too.

"It's all taken care of," he said.

"Holy shit," Abi squealed. "I'm moving to Switzerland!"

We went out for more drinks and more dancing. When he walked me back to my hotel room and I opened the door, his facial expression changed. This calm, collected man I had spent the last twenty-four hours with was gone. He picked me up off my feet, literally swept me off my feet, took me into the bathroom, pushed everything off the counter, slammed me against the mirror, and we made out like we were in eighth grade—but with a lot more skill. We did all kinds of fun things in that bathroom—except have sex. Somehow we both had our reasons to hold back from that final, definitive act. But that man brought my body to the brink more times than I can remember. "I don't want to sleep with you yet," he whispered.

"No . . . no, not yet," I agreed, out of breath and flushed.

"I'm going to see you tomorrow," he said and kissed me good-bye. It was a long, slow, perfect kiss, and I couldn't help thinking back to that first awkward kiss with Michael. Had I been with the wrong person all along? But no, no . . . what was I doing?

After he left, I sat there for a minute on the bathroom counter thinking. I turned to look at myself in the mirror. "What the fuck just happened?" I said out loud.

Abi, who we barely even realized had followed us into the room, peeked into the bathroom and stared at me. "Oh my God, I could hear everything from out here. That was the hottest thing that ever happened to me."

"We didn't have sex," I said.

"What? No way. It sounded like sex."

"It was almost sex. But it wasn't."

"Why not?" She looked baffled. "You're not still thinking of Michael, are you?"

I looked at her guiltily. "Sort of . . ." I admitted. "But something stopped him, too. Something stopped us."

"Maybe he didn't have a condom. Or maybe his dick is crooked. Or inverted or something," she said.

I slid off the counter and threw myself on the bed. "He's definitely not southern," I sighed. The two of us erupted in laughter.

Thomas and I spent the whole next day together, and that night he took me to a company party. He held my hand and introduced me to everyone like I was his girlfriend. It felt so real, so right. At one point, an attractive but severe-looking woman, one of his North American representatives, pulled me aside.

"You can't be here, honey."

"Excuse me?" I said.

"He's the president of one of the largest Swiss companies. I don't know if you're working or what, but you can't be here."

I stared at her. "You think I'm a prostitute?"

"I don't know what you are, but you can't be here."

"I work for a magazine. I'm not a prostitute," I said.

I pushed away from her and found Thomas, and immediately told him what she said. "Fuck her, she's just jealous," he said, and made it a point to parade me past her two or three more times. When she discussed some new technology she found interesting, he turned to me and said, "I don't know. What do you think, Jaime?" It was brilliant and sexy and such a turn-on to be with somebody in such a position of power that he didn't have to worry about what anyone else thought.

After the party, we went outside to watch the fountains at

the Bellagio. As we stood there in the dark with the fountains lit and dancing to the music, he held my hand again and we were quiet for a while, just soaking in the moment and the beauty and the feeling of being together. Finally, he spoke. "We really should just go get married," he said.

I laughed, but felt a little thrill. "Rational people don't do things like that just because they had three great nights together in Vegas," I said.

"That's exactly what rational people do," he said.

"I can't live in Switzerland. I don't even speak your language."

"I speak perfect English," he said.

"Perfect English with a really heavy accent."

Were we really talking about this? I'm not going to lie. I actually thought about it for a second. Why not marry this perfect specimen of a man? He was everything I had always thought I wanted.

"Can you imagine it?" he said, musing.

"I almost can," I said, squeezing his hand. "Almost."

He turned to me. "And why not? We work out all the problems later and they wouldn't matter because we would be together."

"You're a true romantic," I said, and I put my arms around his neck. "I could fall right in love with you and never fall out."

"Then let's do it."

I looked at him for a long, long time. There was no nervous averting of the eyes, no awkwardness, nothing unnatural. It was perfect in that moment . . . but that kind of perfection doesn't last, and I knew it. I think we both did.

Still, I argued with myself in that protracted rapture in front of the fountain. Since when did I even consider what so-called rational people do? Why not go for it? Why not grab the brass ring, take that perfection for myself, let it be mine forever? Why not, why not, why not?

But something still held me back. I think if I'd agreed, we might even have done it—and possibly lived happily ever after . . . or suffered a lifetime of regret. Or a quickie divorce? Who knows? The old Jaime might have jumped right in and gone for it, but this new Jaime, whom I was just getting to know, was holding out for something else—something more real. Something more solid. Something already in her heart. Someone.

The next day, I flew home, unmarried. Thomas and I never slept together, and I went back to Michael, rose-colored glasses cast aside and crushed under my heel. But there was something happening between Michael and me that was slow and beautiful and that I couldn't allow my destructive self to destroy. Maybe it was a rose opening slowly, slowly . . .

Too slowly. I admit I stayed in touch with Thomas. Just in case? I'm not sure. And I loved him, in a different kind of way than I loved Michael. I found myself feeling very connected to both of them. And disconnected from both of them at the same time because there I was, waiting, hanging, and nothing, nothing was happening. And I don't do very well when nothing is happening.

So I decided to make something happen. I did what any confused, fiercely independent woman would do in my situation. If nobody else was going to act, I would. I'd recently had a job offer in Los Angeles that would require actually moving there. I'd been spending more and more time in Birmingham, but . . . maybe the answer really was somewhere else. Or maybe I could force Michael's hand. So I decided to take the job, and actually move to Los Angeles. For real.

I didn't take the job only because I thought it might make Michael reconsider his time line, or to escape memories of Thomas, or to resolve my own issues, or any of that. I did it because it was good for my career, and that was the one and only thing I was sure about. If it lit a fire under Michael, great. If not, maybe it wasn't what I thought it was, and I would be prepared to move on. Besides, I loved LA and I loved the job, which was doing PR for a new restaurant and nightclub.

But I also remembered my mother telling me a story about when she was dating my father. Things were going well, but not progressing fast enough for her liking. So when, after dating for eight months, my father still hadn't made his intentions clear, my mother called him and told him she was moving to Italy to live with her cousins. My father proposed two days later. Like they always say, if it's meant to be, it will be, right? But sometimes, fate can use a boost. I knew it was a risk, but it was a risk I was willing to take.

On the other hand, this sort of thing might work in Jersey, but not necessarily on a man from Alabama. Obviously, I had no earthly idea of what would work on a man from Alabama.

That evening, Michael and I went out for dinner, in our usual way, and I broke the news. I was nervous and excited but I played it cool, almost blasé. The wine arrived, we ordered our food, and I leaned my elbows on the table and looked at him.

"Oh, by the way, I'm leaving for LA in four weeks," I said.

"For how long?" he said.

"Permanently," I said. "I'm moving there."

He paused, his wineglass halfway to his lips. He didn't look at me. He breathed and took a sip. "Yeah, right," he said.

"No, Michael, I'm serious. I'm packing up my apartment in Birmingham, and I'm giving my notice at the magazine, and I'm moving to LA. Full time. It's a great opportunity and I can't pass it up. Besides . . ."

I let that "besides" hang in the air, unfinished.

I watched him closely. He swallowed and looked down at his plate of food as the server set it in front of him. He didn't say anything. I decided that maybe, just maybe, that was a good thing. Maybe he was recognizing that his slow southern ways might not work forever on a Jersey girl who is always in a hurry.

And I did it. I moved to LA.

#cawfeetawk

Bluffs don't always work. They are risky because you can't control what someone else will do when faced with an ultimatum or an extreme situation. Don't ever make a bluff unless you are actually willing to go through with what you say.

– Chapter 9 –

LA WOMAN

$\mathcal{T}$he weirdest thing happened: I moved to LA and I loved it. As an East Coast girl, I never thought I would love the West Coast, but the LA life was unexpectedly *me*. I was killing it in my career. I had great friends. I hung out with celebrities. I was working for one of the most prominent club owners in the biz. I had great clothes and although I wasn't rolling in money, I was doing okay for myself. The weather was gorgeous. The views were stunning. Life was laid-back and cool, and I had respect and status. I *knew people*. It was awesome. It was everything I dreamed about whenever I visited LA for work. I *understood* LA.

But even with all these pieces in place, I was still dating Michael.

I know, you're like, "Waaaaat?"

Somehow, and I'm not sure how he did it, Michael had played off my tactical gambit of moving across the country by making himself more charming and desirable than ever. And so we spent hours on the phone, and we visited each other once a month. I became that LA girl dating a refined southern man. Michael managed to keep my hope alive, but I also think it turned him on that I wasn't hanging around in Birmingham chasing him like so many other women were. I was doing my own thing and I was my own person, and Michael is the kind of guy who likes that in a woman (something his mother liked to remind him was a distinct fault and a major obstacle toward future grandchildren).

Plus, Michael had a way that charmed everyone in LA. Every time he came to visit, my girlfriends flocked around him. The soft-spoken southern gentleman was a real curiosity in LA, and they couldn't get enough. They could totally see why I was dating him, so nobody ever tried to talk me out of it. They loved to ask intimate questions about him. They interrogated me on all things physical, including his sexual skills (as people in LA tend to do). They made me proud to be with him. We were an odd couple for sure, but in a way that had everybody entranced with our story, and with us.

And every so often, he would drop hints. Subtle hints, but hints nonetheless. Like saying, as we walked down the street past a jewelry store, "That's a beautiful ring," or making off-hand comments like, "I don't know about Los Angeles, but maybe someday I'd consider moving to New York City." I didn't know whether he was purposefully stringing me along, or if he was truly exploring possibilities in his own mind. Either way, I didn't push it. I didn't want to scare him away. But I heard it all.

Then one day, my mother called me.

"Jaime!" she yelled through the phone from New Jersey. "Jaime, I have to tell you something, but you have to pretend you don't know!"

My mother keeps a secret like a four-year-old keeps a secret.

I thought it must be some gossip about one of my sisters. I sighed. "What is it this time, Ma?"

"Michael called me and asked my permission to *marry you!*" she said in her thick New York accent. "This is it. I can't *ba-leeeeeeve it!*"

Back the truck up. *What?* "Wait a minute. Did you say he asked your permission? To *marry me?*" I wasn't even annoyed that he felt he had to ask anybody's permission but mine. It was sweet that he asked my mother, since my father had passed away. Sweet as . . . oh, I don't know, southern sweet tea? Oh my God, was I losing my mind?

"Yes!" she crowed. "And I said . . ." She paused for the drama of it. "I said . . . YES!" I could practically hear her grinning.

"You damn well better have, because I would do it anyway!" I said.

"Does that mean you're going to *accept* his *proposal?*" she said, her pitch rising. I could already imagine her planning what she would wear to the wedding.

"I don't know," I said, taking a mental step back. "I guess I'll have to think about it."

"*Jaime!*" she shrieked. "He's a *lovely man!* You *have to marry him!*"

"Ma, you haven't even met him yet. Until a few months ago, you were sure he was gay."

"Enough with the gay. That's over. He's a red-blooded American male, we all know that now! So say yes to the man like a good girl. I've got to go. My shows are coming on."

"Okay. Bye, Ma. I love you."

I hung up the phone and sat for a moment, thinking. Really?

He had asked her? There had been no sign that he was going to do this. So when? *Oh my God, when?*

The problem with knowing somebody is intending to propose is that, every time anything happens, you are just sure it's going to be the moment. Michael was coming to visit me in LA that weekend, and from the second he arrived I read meaning into every single thing he did. When he was washing the dishes and turned around to ask for more soap, I was like, *This is it!* Every time he said, "Hey, babe?" I was like, "Yeeeeeeeeeessss?"

We spent a romantic weekend together, and we hung out with Abi and some of my other friends, dancing and eating good food and having a great time. Like everyone else, Abi loved Michael. I watched his every move, telling no one but waiting, waiting for it to happen. Was his hand going toward his pocket? Was he about to get down on one knee?

But it didn't happen. I was so disappointed. When it was time for him to go back to Birmingham, we stopped at my office before we went to the airport, and he logged into his email to print out his boarding pass. After I dropped him off, I drove back to work. He called me as I was walking into my office.

"We're getting ready to take off. Love you!" he said.

"Love you, too," I said. "Have a safe flight!" I got myself a cup of coffee, mentally prepared to start my day, when I noticed that he had left his email open on my computer.

Now, I know it's none of my business. I shouldn't snoop in anybody else's email. And I didn't snoop, but my eyes just sort of . . . looked. Hmm, maybe there would be some ring purchase information, or something else exciting? A surprise trip?

Instead, I found a conversation between Michael and another woman in Atlanta.

I gawked. I couldn't stop myself from reading it. It was flirty, full of innuendo. It didn't sound like Michael at all. And yet, there it was with his name signed at the end. There they were, the kinds of words I always longed to hear from him. He wasn't flirty and full of innuendo in our texts and emails. *Who is he?* I began to panic. *Who is this man who supposedly wants to marry me but is flirting in a free-and-easy way I never get to see with some woman I've never even heard of?*

My whole word came crashing down. I had been willing to give up everything. My job, my career, my friends, my life in LA, the red carpets, the parties, the excitement, the glamour. I was mentally prepared to throw it all away for a man who could so breezily tell another woman that he would *love to catch up and maybe even* . . .

Dot-dot-dot. The dreaded, suggestive, maddening ellipsis. What the fuck did he mean by dot-dot-dot? I wanted to scream. I wanted to cry. I wanted to throw the computer out the window. Instead, I took a slow, deep breath and said out loud, "Jaime, you need to talk to him."

But he was on a plane, and would be on a plane for four and a half hours. So I called Michael's brother Father Bob.

Michael's brother is a priest, and he was the one sibling I had spent the most time with, though occasionally and informally. He was a kind man with a good sense of humor, and I immediately loved him like a brother. I felt a special kinship to him, especially since I had converted to Catholicism in my early twenties. I'd never called him with a problem before, but I did have his number in my phone, so I dialed it.

"Father Bob?" I said, my voice wavering. And then I burst into tears.

"Jaime? Are you okay?" said Father Bob, obviously perplexed by my dry heaving.

The floodgates opened. I told him everything. I cried and screamed and cursed and he listened and tried to talk me down from the ledge.

"Jaime, I'm sure it's nothing. I'm sure it was harmless. I'm not making excuses, but I know for a fact my brother loves you."

"I can't believe I was willing to uproot my whole fucking life for him!" I said.

"Don't throw it all away, Jaime," Father Bob said. "This is a mistake."

Finally, I let him go, and my boss walked in to the office. He was young, rich, and very LA-hip, and he had no interest in seeing me cry. He took one look at me and said, "Train wreck. What's happening? Never mind, I don't want to know. Go home. Get out of my office."

I called Abi on the way home. She met me at my apartment, crawled into bed with me, and played with my hair while I cried for three hours and left Michael a series of angry, hysterical messages. Why shouldn't he have his own ugly surprise, like the one he'd given me? I called him names. I told him it was over. I told him I could never trust him again. I just didn't tell him why.

Between calls, Abi said soothing things to me like, "Jaime, that's not the Michael we know. There has to be an explanation. Don't do anything rash. You need to talk to him first. The real Michael is wonderful. The real Michael loves you."

"The real Michael is a lying cheating son of a bitch!" I yelled, until I was too tired to yell anymore, and all I could do was cry quietly into my pillow.

But even after Abi left and I had calmed down externally, my mind couldn't stop churning out horrible scenarios of doom. *This is why I don't ever want to wait for someone to get down on one knee. This is why I run first. This is why I don't believe in happily ever after. Because it doesn't fucking exist.* I blamed everybody who had ever said anything nice about Michael. They had led me down this road, to believe in this shit. They had filled my head with what a great guy he was and how amazing he was. Now I knew the truth: Men are like dogs. They may look cute and act loyal, but they can still bite, and the second you stop remembering that is the second when you get hurt. And I was just so hurt. So, so hurt. Even if he hadn't actually done anything with that woman, I decided the fact that he could send her an email like that told me everything I ever needed to know about men.

I was also angry at myself because it was my own fault that I'd let my old reliable defense system go down. I had let it come down for him, and sure, romantic people might say, *That's life and you take chances. That's love. Better to have loved and lost than never to have* . . . Bullshit! It was all bullshit! I had been doing just fine getting marriage proposals from hot Swiss guys in front of awe-inspiring fountains at lavish hotels. I was not lacking romance in my life. I was not hurting for grand gestures. I was not a wallflower who had no interest from the outside world. I was a strong, powerful career woman with the world at my feet. So why was I lying here, vulnerable? How could I have let this happen? My weakness was represented right there in that email, in that fucking dot-dot-dot.

Up until Michael, I had doubted everything about everyone. Do you know what that's like, to live like that? To doubt every person's intentions? To never, ever fully believe that anyone means what they say? I had been disappointed so many times in my life that I never took anyone at face value. My high school boyfriend, whom I loved more than anything in the world, slept with my best friend. My mother promised me my father would get better, and he died. Relationship after relationship had been a disappointment. The reason I do so much for myself and never ask for help, I realized, is because nobody else has ever come through for me.

Until I met Michael. Michael was the first relationship I had ever been in where it didn't even occur to me that the man I was with could ever betray me. Sure, he was too old for me. Too southern. Too mature. Sure, he liked *Macbeth* and I liked Stephen King. He liked to go to the symphony and I liked classic hip-hop. Sometimes he was even a little boring, but those were the only hurdles I thought we would ever have. Now those seemed less like hurdles and more like horrible waving red flags I had completely refused to see. Now I felt like screaming at myself: *You fool, Jaime! You are such a fool. You let yourself believe, if only for one second, that there might be somebody out there who is what he says he is. And now you know that you were weak and gullible. Now you know that nobody like that really exists.*

As soon as he landed, my phone rang. His voice was frantic. "What is it? What's wrong?" he said.

I was calmer than I ever remembered being before. "You left your email up," I said, my voice a monotone. "And I looked because I'm human. And I saw your message to her." I read it to him out loud, emphasizing the *dot-dot-dot*.

He was gutted. I could hear it in his voice. "I'm going to tell you the true story of what happened right now," he said. "She's someone from the past. She emailed me out of nowhere when I was in Montgomery for legislative session, just a casual, 'Hey, how's session, are you coming to Atlanta anytime soon?' She did not know I was in a committed relationship. She flirted, I flirted back over the course of a few emails, and when she said we should get together to catch up the next time I was in Atlanta, that's what I wrote. I know it was wrong, but it didn't mean anything. I never had any intention of following through with it. I never saw her. There was no more correspondence after that email. That doesn't make it right, but it's not what you think."

"Yes, Michael. It is what I think. It is exactly what I think, because I put you on a pedestal. I made you perfect in my mind, and guess what? You're not perfect. You're human like everybody else. I don't care what you actually did or didn't do because now I know the truth about what is in your mind, and that's what matters. This is just another disappointment in a long string of disappointments in my life, and I'm not going to do this anymore. So it's over."

I hung up and I called Leigh Anne and asked her to go to pick up the stuff I was keeping at Michael's place. Because we were doing this. This was happening. He had already asked for my mother's permission to marry me and I had my stuff at his house, but none of that mattered now. I was putting an end to it. Because oh my God, he was in his fucking forties! In my world, that was practically an artifact. He was clearly too old for me. And clearly too old to be a player. I was used to dating guys in their late twenties, and I knew *they* were players, but I would never have expected it of Michael.

Later that night, Father Bob called me. "For whatever it's worth, my brother is heartbroken," he told me. "He never meant to hurt you and he still loves you very much. I'll pray for both of you."

"Don't pray for me. Pray for him," I said. "I'm good."

"Be careful, Jaime," he said. "That's not you. That's the old Jaime."

"And she's *welcome back*," I said, hanging up the phone. What did he know about the "old Jaime"? The old Jaime knew how to protect herself. I cried myself to sleep.

The next morning, after barely sleeping, I woke up with puffy eyes to an email from Michael: *You know what? You probably dodged a bullet. I'm a bad egg. Everything I told you about that woman is true, and it meant nothing to me. But overall, you're probably lucky. I'm damaged goods.*

I raged, *What an easy way out for you, Michael Sullivan, with your fucking bullets and dodging bullshit. Don't you dare write me an email basically quietly bowing out stage left. Don't you dare let yourself off the hook like that.*

I was still fighting for him.

And it hit me. It was the most obvious thing in the world.

Why hadn't I seen it before? *I wasn't the only one coming into this relationship damaged and with insecurities and defenses and walls and baggage and a history of heartache.* I read his email over a few times and it was all so clear: He was terrified, too. Even though Michael always has such a calm sense of self about him, he was just as scared about what was coming as I was.

I also saw something even more obvious: How could I really fault him for entertaining a little flirtation in an email when I had briefly pondered an actual marriage proposal in Vegas? He sent me that rose-colored-glasses text, but wasn't I saying the same thing to him by my behavior? We were both petrified of commitment, even though we both wanted to be together. We were in the same boat. In this central facet, we were the same.

I wanted him. I still wanted him. Despite the pain and the fear and the hurt, I wanted him.

I swallowed my enormous pride, and I called him. "Michael. Look," I said, without giving him a chance to say anything. "We're both fucked up. But I'd rather be fucked up together than apart. So I'm going to do something for you that I've never done for anyone. I'm not going to run. I'm going to let this go, and never bring it up again."

He was quiet for a moment. Then he said, "I've never been extended that kind of grace by another human being."

"I love you, Michael."

"Jaime, I love you, too."

And that, as they say, was that. We were back on, and better than ever. When we were together, it was with a new level of intimacy and tenderness. I felt his love, more palpably than I had before, and I made sure that he felt mine. We could help each other heal. I knew that now.

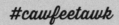

#cawfeetawk

The old saying "Love means never having to say you're sorry" is total bullshit. Love means having to say you are sorry all the time, and meaning it, and then moving on together despite each other's mistakes. We all have baggage and when we act outside of our true nature because we are clinging to old pain, that behavior requires an apology.

Chapter 10

YANKEE IMPATIENCE AND THE QUEST FOR THE RING

I was still waiting for that proposal. It must be coming. If he had had doubts before, surely they were dispelled. We were bonded forever. Weren't we? He was sure of it. Wasn't he?

Two weeks later, we were going to a friend's wedding in Augusta, Georgia, in mid-May. This was obviously the perfect setting, and I hoped against hope that this might finally seal the deal. I was tired of waiting and I wanted the proof that we were a sure thing. I just had this feeling that this trip would provide the perfect moment. Then again, I had been pretty sure he would kiss me on the third date—I still wasn't entirely confident about the whole southern courtship timeline. Or was it the over-forty-bachelor timeline? Whatever it was, I was still confused.

But the weekend would be the perfect opportunity. Surely he saw that. So I prepared. I packed my sexiest lingerie, my best underwear, the clothes I knew he loved on me. We met in Birmingham and drove to Georgia together, and I was witty and funny and complimentary and practically batting my eyelashes in an attempt to inspire whatever courage he might require to propose to me. We spent a great weekend together in a romantic hotel room, and I was a dynamo. Attentive and sweet and wild in bed, too. I did every single thing I'd ever read about in *Cosmo*. He could barely keep up with me.

On Sunday morning, after the wedding was over, we woke up in the hotel room and he got up to take a shower, and I was getting desperate. There wasn't much time left. I leapt out of bed and I tore that room apart. I just knew there had to be a ring somewhere. It wasn't too late! We were still there! The trip wasn't over yet! And I wanted to know it was coming so I could be mentally prepared.

But I couldn't find it! There was no sign of a ring anywhere. Finally I called my sister Meredith. "There's got to be a ring here somewhere," I whispered, listening to make sure the shower was still running.

"Look harder!"

"It's got to be here," I said. "Seriously, I sucked his balls. Both balls. I even did the humming thing. It's got to be here."

"Find the fucking ring!" she said.

But there was no ring to be found. Finally, I gave up, deciding it must not be happening on this trip. Either that or he'd hidden it in a body cavity. And even then, at the rate I'd been going, I probably would have found it.

On our way back to the airport, where Michael was dropping me off so I could fly back to Los Angeles, I had given up. I sat pouting, staring out the window, barely talking, exhausted from efforts that hadn't paid off. Then the capitol building in Atlanta came into view. Michael pulled his car over to the side of the road. It was May in Atlanta, which means it was ninety degrees and about 475 percent humidity. You could have wrung me out like a sponge. I was disgusting, but Michael made me get out of the car anyway.

"Really? In this heat? Do I have to?" I whined.

"Come here. I want to show you something." He took my hand and pulled me along the winding sidewalk up toward the capitol.

Now, you have to understand that Michael is a lobbyist, and lobbyists get really excited about things like the new paint on the side of a federal building, or a plaque marking some historical moment, or a statue of some old white guy with a beard. That's what I was expecting. *Kill me now.* I tried to smile with interest, but couldn't help adding, "Michael, I'm sweating like a pig. Can we get back in the car?"

"Just come with me for a minute," he said, dragging me farther down the sidewalk. Sure enough, we stopped at a plaque about southern history and he read it to me out loud. I rolled my eyes. He took me to the next plaque and read that one. Then the next one. By this time I am bored out of my mind and sweating under my bra. Now I'm thinking, *I have to get on a plane with boob sweat?* I was barely listening to him at all. I was too busy visualizing cold showers and tall glasses of lemonade so I wouldn't pass out. Then, out of nowhere, he started to clutch on me. And Michael is not a clutcher.

"What are you doing?" I said in exasperation. I wanted to slap his hands away. I was at that level of hot-and-sticky where I didn't want anyone to look at me, let alone touch me. Then he began to sink to the ground. *OMG*, I thought, . . . *he's going down like a sack of potatoes. I'm going to have to call an ambulance.*

And then I realized he was down on one knee. Oh shit. No

way. Here? Now? With boob sweat? I looked around helplessly at passersby who were beginning to slow down and watch. *Surely my marriage proposal is not going to go down in front of the capitol building in Atlanta.* I couldn't think of a less romantic spot, but he was on a trajectory and there was no stopping him. A crowd was forming. Why was I the only one sweating? *Fucking southern people, they stand cooking in the sun and they don't even seem to notice the heat!*

I looked down at Michael, a drop of sweat shimmering on the end of my nose, and I blinked.

"I love you very much," he said. "I was a broken bird before you came into my life, and now I am healed. I never knew I could love someone the way I love you. Will you marry me?"

I didn't hesitate. Suddenly the sun didn't matter. The crowd didn't matter. And the Georgia State Capitol seemed like the most romantic spot in the whole world.

"Yes!" I said, pulling him up and throwing my arms around him. He put the ring on my finger and kissed me and everyone around us clapped. It felt surreal. All of a sudden, I was different than I was before.

We stopped at a restaurant to toast and call his parents and just before he dropped me off at the airport, he said, "So, you need to put everybody on notice that you're moving to Alabama. I think August is a good time. That gives you two months to tie up loose ends." He kissed me good-bye.

"What? Wait . . . what?" I said. He smiled, squeezed my hand, and drove away, leaving me with a suitcase and a head full of questions.

I boarded the plane, zombie-like. Put everyone on notice?

Loose ends? Moving away? Suddenly I realized what the proposal had been all about. To him, the Georgia State Capitol was a symbol—that I was to become part of his world, his life, the South. He was welcoming me into his world, in the best way he knew how, reading me those plaques that meant so much to him, that depicted the history of the place that was soon to be mine.

I was about to go native. Because we were getting married.

It was everything I thought I wanted, and everything I didn't want, all at the same time.

#cawfeetawk

Everything we go through is either a test or a lesson. Do not allow either to block the blessings meant for you. Extend grace. Practice forgiveness. And always do the humming thing. XO

Chapter 11

THE GREATEST LOVE
STORY EVER TOLD

So I was engaged to the love of my life. But he wasn't my greatest love. Let me explain.

I am Catholic now, but I was born and raised Jewish. My grandparents were Catholic, and so was my mother, until she converted for my father and embraced the role with the fervor of any natural-born Jersey Jew. I was raised in a Jewish household and I even had a fancy-schmancy bat mitzvah with a carnival theme. So how did I transform from that little Jersey Jew to the woman who called a priest in her time of need?

The answer is truly the greatest love story ever told. It began long before I met the man of my dreams. It was a circuitous path and it was not a pursuit by me for something higher. It was a pursuit by Him to win me over. But I didn't make it easy for Him.

My context and everything I knew was a sort of Jersey-style secular Judaism. One of my earliest memories is the sound of mah-jongg tiles. I remember waking up at one in the morning to the clinking and sliding of those tiles as they were swirled around on the fold-out card table by my mother and her three friends who obsessively played this game. They were often together, and they were usually around that card table—and they were four of the loudest Jersey Jews you've ever heard.

"Who ate the last of the lox?"

"How do I know?"

"What, you need more lox? It's one o'clock in the morning!"

This was my childhood household. It was loud. It was open. It was over-the-top. It usually involved food, and it was ruled by my mother.

My mother was a stunner. An absolute knockout. She had big boobies and big Jersey hair. She was from Manhattan and she always had an air of privilege about her. She wasn't from the uppermost upper crust, but her family was well connected and when you met her, you knew it. She didn't have to mention it. She was this juicy, captivating blend of sophistication and vulgarity, as if she could say and do whatever she wanted because she was so confident about her place in the world.

My mother smoked cigarettes like it was the most fabulous thing a woman could do with her mouth. This fascinated me. I used to take candy cigarettes out of the box and practice my smoking and talking with it dangling out of my lips like my mother would do when she was on the phone. Every once in a while I would take a drag and hold it in, as if I was considering the best way to say something very profound. At the time, all the serious health risks associated with smoking weren't common knowledge, so my mother thought my candy cigarette habit was great practice for life. When we had company, she would wave her hand at me.

"Jaime, go get your candy cigarettes and show everybody what you can do!"

And although they were, for all intents and purposes, both Jewish, my parents' temperaments were diametrically opposed. While my mother would prefer to drink vodka and have a wild time with her friends, my father preferred to kick back with a joint and watch *Jeopardy!* Their differences extended to every corner of their relationship, but despite their differences, oh boy did my father love my mother. None of us ever doubted that. I remember as a rebellious teenager, begging my father to divorce my mother and take me to live with him in a different house. He always had the same answer.

"I'm not going to divorce your mom, Jaime."

"But why? She's a lunatic!"

"She is," he would agree with a smile. "But that's why I love her."

I grew up going to Hebrew school, and from an early age I believed everybody was Jewish. Even though my grandparents weren't—they were Italian Catholic in every sense of the word—truthfully, I didn't really understand the difference. I just thought Catholic meant my grandmother had taken some amazing cooking classes and gotten some kind of special status. I knew that we celebrated Christmas at Grandma's house but I didn't understand why she celebrated Christmas and we didn't. But I didn't question. Because . . . presents!

Christmas was the one thing my mother had a hard time letting go of. At first, she told my father, "You can't have Hanukkah without a Christmas tree."

"Yes, actually, you can," he said.

"Well then, what about this nice white tree. It isn't actually a Christmas tree. Christmas trees are green. This is . . . it's a Hanukkah bush."

My father didn't even look at the tree she had optimistically set up in the living room. "No, it's not. It's a white Christmas tree." In the interest of familial stability, we all decided that my mother's white Christmas tree could, if you squinted and turned your head a certain way, look almost like a Hanukkah bush. The tree stayed. Right next to the menorah.

My mother's Hanukkah bush compromise is just one example of her stubborn, not necessarily logical passion toward life in general. Sometimes this passion manifested as excessive exuberance, and sometimes it was all about certain doom, loudly expressed. Although extravagant, nothing she did had any particular rhyme or reason to it, but there was always heart and noise involved. Susan Primak was big and bold, boisterous and beautiful, and everything I learned about entertaining and social skills (for better or worse), I learned from her.

When we had people over for food, the serving bowls and utensils never matched. There were no monogrammed napkins or any particular social graces, but there was love in the food, reflected by the size of the spread. Even when she was setting up for her weekly card game, I remember marveling at the smorgasbord of Jewish gems: bagels and cream cheese, lox and capers and red onions, knishes and kugel, latkes and rugelach. My childhood was exciting and delicious and to me, that was what being an Italian Jew (a so-called pizza bagel) was all about.

You Might Be a Jew from Jersey if . . .

- You spend Christmas Day seeing a movie then going for Chinese.
- You eat Chinese every Sunday night.
- You're only religious on the High Holy Days.
- You legitimately love latkes *and* pizza.
- You know how to cook a brisket *and* make a killer marinara.
- You'll eat a deep-fat-fried hot dog topped with bacon, but you will never, ever eat ham.
- You shopped at Smith Bros, Pants Place, or Merry-Go-Round.
- You wore Hotdoggers, Cavaricci's, Wigwam socks, scrunchies, and Hypercolor T-shirts.
- You see someone get lifted up on a chair and it seems normal to you.
- You've seen a Guido wearing a yarmulke and understood what you were seeing.

But for me, being a Jew was never really about being spiritual. We only went to temple on High Holy Days, and I didn't pray. When I left for college at seventeen, I took my Judaism, but not any faith, along with me. I had nothing to support me or sustain me in the wake of my father's death other than my own anger and rebellion and strong personality. They served me well enough, but after I graduated and began to move around, I began to feel more and more adrift.

In my new life as a young adult, relationships kept failing. Friendships kept fading. And oddly enough, I kept meeting

Christians who seemed happy and sure of themselves, and who kept urging me, in all kinds of strange and disparate contexts, to go to church with them. College roommates, hip-hop friends, girls I met at parties, and the occasional older adult would seemingly randomly bring up religion and ask me, "What do you believe?" I would laugh at them. I would even mock them. I would make fun of Jesus. I would remind them I was Jewish. I would scorn them, but they kept coming, as if God were sending an assembly line of invitations to know Him.

It was the children that finally got to me. When I was teaching high school in Jersey City, some of my students convinced me to go with them to church, and after much youthful and innocent coercion, I agreed, not wanting to disappoint them. I didn't tell anybody I was going. I sat in the back, alone, listening. Those secretive church services spoke to me, but I still considered myself a Jew. I was cross-training. Or something. I was experimenting, maybe. I was Christian-curious. Whatever it was, I found it deeply satisfying and moving, but I felt I could never tell any of my friends or family about my clandestine liaisons with Jesus.

There was a time in my early twenties when I was at the rock bottom of a failed relationship. It was truly the lowest point in my life. I was emotionally, mentally, and physically broken. I was completely alone and contemplating ending it all. It was in that moment that God finally spoke to me, directly, intervening in my life when I needed Him the most. I guess He was tired of sending me hints, of waiting for me to come to Him.

And I mean it literally when I say He spoke to me. I know how it sounds, but I'll never forget the moment it happened.

It was one of those dark nights I spent alone on the bathroom floor, sobbing and believing my life was meaningless. I was lost. I could barely remember the carefree Jaime I was as a child, or the wild partying Jaime I was in college. All I knew was this desperate, grasping, hysterical, sad Jaime who had gone so horribly off course. I didn't know where to turn anymore. I'd left everyone in my life, friends and family, and I felt completely alone. I remember sitting on that cold tile floor and saying out loud: "Why? Why me? Why me? What happened to me?" It was my dark night of the soul. I was pouring myself out because I couldn't hold it in anymore. And then, all of a sudden, there was a voice. It was inside my head, but it was not me. I could hear it clearly. It said:

Don't you get it? I'm right here.

At first I ignored it. I was feeling crazy. I was out of my head. It was nothing. It was my imagination. "I can't do this by myself anymore!" I wailed. "I can't get through this!"

And then, the voice again. *All you have to do is choose me. All you have to do is turn around and see me.*

I stopped crying. I listened. I even turned around to look behind me. But I knew who it was. I think God knew I would never survive on my own, and after years of bread-crumb trails and polite invitations, He knew He was going to have to be more obvious.

All you have to do is make the choice to see me.

I stood up slowly and I looked in the mirror, and the change was instantaneous. It hit me like a bolt of lightning. You know that line from the song "Amazing Grace": "Was blind, but now I see"? I saw. I saw Him, right there, within me, and I got it.

And I knew I would never go back. I knew beyond a shadow of a doubt that He was there, fighting for me, loving me, praying for me, screaming for me, sending soldier after soldier to get my attention. Finally, He had it. And in that exact second, I had accountability. For the first time in my life. I felt like my breath had been taken away. In that second, my life changed. I no longer lived just for myself. In that second, I became acutely aware of all the things I had ever done to other people. Remorse and guilt descended on me. I realized I could have done better. I should have done better. *I would do better.*

I didn't know how I would do better, and I wouldn't grow into my relationship with God for years, but in that moment, at my weakest, when I wanted to die, I was finally able to turn around and say, *I see you now.*

The next morning, I still felt Him. I was different, permanently changed, but I had to make it official. I was compelled. The next step was to join the church and sign up for RCIA classes. "Rite of Christian Initiation of Adults" is basically a class for people who want to convert to Catholicism. I went through with it, and I got confirmed as a Catholic on Easter Sunday 2004. My mom came, and she was truly happy for me. For personal reasons, she wanted me to stay Jewish, but she also understood. She grew up Catholic herself, and she couldn't deny the profound change in me. She also saw that I finally had a way to deal with my anger and hurt, and no mother wants her child to hurt.

To ease her mind, I assured her that I wasn't giving up my Jewish cultural heritage. Once a Jew, always a Jew, and I will always honor my father and where he came from, but after he died, it didn't help me. Christianity and Catholicism in particular became, for me, the thing my life was missing—the spirituality I had longed for without realizing it, that had pursued me and won me over.

After that, I changed my life. I ended the hurtful abusive relationship and moved into my own place, and from that moment everything in my life that was meant to be began to happen quickly. One week later, I ran into Michael for the second time, in the same café. It was God who led me back to Michael. Of this I have no doubt.

I go to church on Sundays, and I pray daily, but the most important part of my faith is love. I love God. I still have days of deep struggle, but I love God, and I know God loves me, and that makes everything different. I have seen His grace. Nobody can take that away from me.

God fought battles to get to me. He took me down roads paved with heartache so that I would see Him. He continued to come for me even after I rejected Him and laughed in His face, even when I thought I knew that God was for everyone else but not for me. I thought that wasn't who I was, and I knew that wasn't how I was raised. I had already denounced Him and made every excuse for why He could not and would not be a part of my life.

But God is stubborn and persistent and even more tenacious than I am. He came with quiet fury. He came to me over and over. He was not going to stop until He got my attention. He was not going to let me live a life that was a walk in the park, because people who truly need God aren't walking through any parks. They aren't musing to themselves, *Hmm, this rose smells nice. I think I'll accept Jesus as my Lord and Savior.* No, you have to realize you can't put your faith in any human being. You have to realize you have nothing and you are nothing. Only then can you see that because He is in you, that you are everything. That you are beloved.

Have you ever had a friend who wanted to be more than a friend, and you were like, "No way, I've been friends with him for years. No way, he dated my girlfriend. No way, I hate the way he chews his food." And one day, you think . . . *Well, maybe. Well . . . what if? Maybe one date.* And you go on that one date, and he kisses you, and you're thinking, *Huh. That wasn't so bad.* And before you know it, you're madly in love?

This was like that. I was madly in love with God. He saved me. There was not another person I met after that day, not another man that I loved, not another road that I traveled, that didn't lead me in the right direction. God was coming for me, calling for me, sending for me. There was no move I made after that that He was not standing right in front of me.

I'm the first one to admit I'm still ultimately flawed. I've done a lot of things that people could point to and say, "That's not Christian." I still make plenty of mistakes. I still curse constantly but I can still love God while saying the F-word. And if you know me, you know that I am exactly that combination of opposing forces. But God didn't come into my life to make me perfect. He loves me despite my flaws. *Because of my flaws.* And every day, I try to be better for Him.

God also didn't come to me so that I would walk around and quote scripture. That's not what He needs from me. He didn't save me to become a preacher. That's not my calling. My calling is to love other people back to life for exactly who they are, and to let them know that we are all works in progress. And that all we have to do is love ourselves because this will allow us to love other people. I'm no Bible-beater. I'm just a believer who has lived life both ways, and discovered which way works better for me.

Most important, God gave me all the tools I would need for my Southern Education that was yet to come. Christianity became the one thing I could understand about the South. God is strong below the Mason-Dixon, and now that made sense to me. When I didn't understand anyone and no one understood me, God was our common language, and that saved my life.

So as I was about to move to Alabama and change everything, I held on tight to my faith. I had no idea what was in store for me. He brought me to my knees, and sent me to Michael, and then He said:

Look at me. Because what is about to happen to you is going to be amazing and you can't do it without me.

And He was so right.

#cawfeetawk

Romans 9:28–33: God doesn't count us; he calls us by name. *Amen.*

Chapter 12

"SURELY NOT"

And so I began the change, from single girl to fiancée, from commitment-phobe to legitimately engaged woman. From Jersey girl to . . . what? What was I going to be now? *Southern?* Slowly I began to tell people in Los Angeles, mostly when they noticed the ring on my finger. The common response, completely the opposite of when they met Michael, was, "What the hell are you thinking? Alabama? Your career is *over!*"

And I believed them. There I was, enjoying increasing success, loving LA, and finally making a name for myself in the PR field. And now I was going to move back to Alabama and actually *live there*? Throw it all away and be *a wife*? It had all moved so slowly, and now it was all going so fast. People kept asking me about it. *Why, why, WHY?* I just wanted to stand up and scream, *Can everybody please just give me a minute?*

I didn't need help worrying about this. Whenever I thought about living in Alabama, I almost had a panic attack. I continually calmed myself with thoughts of Michael. *Michael knows best. Michael is the one. Michael has a vision for our lives. Michael has a plan. He must have a plan.*

But I already knew I wouldn't fit in. I didn't stand a chance. I had convinced myself of it, and what we tell ourselves becomes our truth. I had enough experience with Alabama to know I was a fish out of water. Or more like a *knish out of water*. Those weren't my people. I knew it even before Michael called his mother from Atlanta, right after he proposed. "Mother," he said from the restaurant where we went to celebrate, "I want you to know that I've asked Jaime to marry me."

"Oh." There was a long silence. She was literally speechless. "Hold on, let me get your father." She put him on the line and went away to deal with the news in her own way.

Michael's mother and I both knew that I wasn't her people.

When two people get engaged, of course, one of the first sobering things that happens is The Meeting of the Families. I had already met Michael's family, but he had never met mine. He never actually *said* he was dreading his obligatory trip to New Jersey to meet my family, but how could he not? Anyway, fair was fair.

When I first met my future mother-in-law, I thought, *This has to be a joke, right?* Oh, don't feel too sorry for her. I'm quite sure she was thinking exactly the same thing about me. It was after one of our "church dates" in Birmingham, but long before Michael ever proposed. Michael and I met both his parents for breakfast at a beautiful restaurant with white tablecloths and real silver and china teacups for coffee. We sat outside under a massive yellow umbrella that shielded us from the Alabama sunshine, and I remember talking about how I was raised Jewish but converted to Catholicism. The conversion earned me points—Michael's mother is *very* Catholic, so I had that going for me.

But I think those were the only points I got. I could tell I was being observed, the way a judge observes a gymnastics competition, noting every slip. Carole is the oldest of nine children, including seven boys, whom she basically raised as a sensible and competent older sister. Then she had five sons. She had spent most of her life bringing up boys, so I felt like I was auditioning for the role of the daughter she never had—and failing miserably. I was *nothing* like any daughter Carole Sullivan would ever raise. Every time I talked, she raised her eyebrows, as if the very sound of my Jersey accent distressed her (and it probably did). I began to feel very self-conscious. Every move I made, every word I spoke, seemed to be wrong. Was I using the right fork? Was my napkin arranged in my lap correctly? Did I eat too much? At least I didn't make the mistake of trying to hug her! God forbid.

As she sipped her coffee and daintily tasted her eggs, I realized that although she was alien to me, she reminded me of Michael. Neither of them is very demonstrative or needs much in the way of emotion or outward displays of affection. I bond with physicality, and I had broken through Michael's barriers, but I couldn't figure out how to relate to his mother. We couldn't get in sync, and although she watched me carefully, she also didn't seem very interested in anything I had to say.

What did interest her were "my people."

"Tell me about your family, Jaime."

I was tongue-tied. What about my family could possibly impress her? She is the quintessential southern belle and I saw right from the beginning that I would never measure up to what she wanted me to be. No way. Because Carole is not just southern. She is the very *best* of what southern can be. I could see that she was poised and proper and she valued tradition and etiquette and everything good that represents the southern woman. I would soon learn that there were things she believed every woman should know, like how to sew on a button, how to fix a zipper, how to bake a perfect chocolate chip cookie, and how to set a proper dinner table. (I knew exactly zero of these things.) She was petite and small-boned with beautiful blue eyes and a soft voice. She actually keeps aprons hanging on a hook in her kitchen for when she cooks. Her go-to F-bomb is *fiddlesticks*.

My mom's F-bomb is the more traditional one. She's robust. She walks into a room and her whole ass waves hello, so Carole was definitely not what I was accustomed to. Michael calls his mother "Mother." I call my mother "Ma," which drives him crazy, but what kind of person actually calls their mother "Mother" without being ironic? My mother never made us feel like women needed to know any of that domestic stuff. She had other lessons for me, like "You go out there and win at whatever you do," and "If you need to fight, I don't care who started it, you finish it." Those were my Jersey lessons, and meeting Carole gave me the distinct impression that my Alabama lessons would prove to be altogether different.

So yes, there were differences. Vast cultural divides, in fact.

But if I knew I had a hard road ahead with my future mother-in-law, I also knew that Jersey was not the place for Michael. Michael grew up in a house with order and purpose. Every plate had a place and every cup had a saucer. When Michael's mother bothered to open her mouth and speak actual words, there was always a good reason. Michael's family didn't watch TV, was not exposed to pop culture, and none of those five boys were ever allowed to raise their voices. So if I was uncomfortable in his world, he could at least gain some sympathy by experiencing a little discomfort in mine. After all, my family was about to be his family, too. I knew coming to Jersey would be serious culture shock for my future husband. But it was a test he had to pass—or at the very least, show up to take.

The first thing my mother boomed through the phone as we called her from that same Atlanta restaurant was, "When is he coming to Jersey? Michael, when are you coming to *Jersey*?!" I bought the tickets right away. This was something I *couldn't wait to witness*.

As soon as we landed, we rented a car and drove toward my sister Meredith's house. Michael's eyes remained transfixed on the Jersey Turnpike: smoke billowing from stacks, horns honking, and music thumping from speakers as cars whipped in and out of lanes. I watched him as he took it all in. He looked terrified. I couldn't help but smile. Finally, a taste of his own medicine. As we approached Meredith's front door, you could hear the noise before we even rang the doorbell. We paused on the doorstep, and I looked at Michael. "Are you ready for this?" I said.

"Is something wrong in there?" he asked, clearly a little concerned.

"No, that's just the normal family noise," I said.

"Surely not," he said.

"You better believe it."

Any house inhabited by any member of my family will automatically be a chaotic hodgepodge of people all speaking over one another, most of them with food in their mouths. We are the worst mess of ADD-riddled people you've ever seen, and nobody can stay on one subject or on track for more than a few minutes, but everyone is always just so excited to be in the same room with everyone else. We are a loud and messy bunch, but the dominant energy and mood in my family home has always been one of love and laughter and reminiscing and storytelling.

I introduced Michael to my mother, who was already in the kitchen tasting the sauce Meredith was making. "Michael!" she shrieked. "My new *son* is here! Look, everybody, it's *Michael*!" She barreled over and hugged him and slapped him on the back vigorously. "Hello, *son*! Welcome to our humble home!" He smiled weakly. I was proud that he didn't run away at that moment, though I'm sure I saw his eyes noting the nearest exit.

Meredith was cooking a big dinner, so after introductions she asked if we could go pick up a few things at the supermarket. Michael looked relieved and turned toward the door like a rat that had just discovered his way out of a maze. My brother, David, sauntered into the room, shook Michael's hand with a Jersey level of friendly violence, and punched him on the shoulder.

"I'll come with you!" he said. I hugged him. I couldn't have been happier to see my baby brother. But I was also worried. Michael and David in the same car, within the first five minutes of arriving in Jersey? I had thought I might ease him in a little more gradually.

David and I talked nonstop in the car and Michael said nothing. He drove, his eyes fixed on the road. I couldn't read his face. Every time I tried to include him in the conversation, he gave me a startled look, as if I was speaking in another language and he had no idea what I was talking about.

In the supermarket, Michael went off with the cart to find some things while David and I stood in the pasta aisle gabbing.

"What's up with him?" David said. "I feel like he's silently judging me. And why is he so quiet?"

"You met him five minutes ago," I said. "Just give him a chance."

"He's kind of an old man," he said.

"Shut up."

"Is he going to say *Howdy, pardner?* Are banjos going to play?"

"That's so original," I said. "I've never heard that one before."

"Seriously," he said. "He looks like he stepped out of a Brooks Brothers catalog. And what's with that hair? And why are his jeans pulled up to his waist?"

"Why are you wearing a wife beater?" I said.

"Because I've got *style*," he said.

Just then, as Michael came around the corner and started walking down the aisle, I saw it. It was happening in slow motion and there was nothing I could do. David lifted one leg, turned his ass in Michael's direction, and farted. I reached out, a slow-motion "Noooooooo!" coming out of my mouth. Michael's face contorted in horror. He was trapped in a cloud of embarrassment and whatever Italian sub sandwich David had eaten a couple of hours before. As the smoke cleared, Michael caught his breath, put his arm around me, and whispered:

"Surely not."

"Welcome to Jersey," I said.

After dinner, my mother insisted on showing home movies. I think she wanted to see just how much Michael could take. They were goading him, I could tell, but in a loving way. They knew if Michael was going to marry me, this is what he would have to deal with. Scene after scene of our family yelling through the decades was clearly disturbing to Michael. He kept looking from the TV to the real live family around him, in some kind of mix of awe and horror. I could practically hear him thinking: *Clearly nothing has changed.* We all laughed hysterically at the video of David pooping in his potty for the first time. Little two-year-old David stood up and yelled, "I'm done!"

"Surely not," Michael murmured, as much to himself as to me.

That night, Michael went into the bathroom to take a shower and I sat on the bed with Meredith, catching up on everything we hadn't yet covered in both of our lives. And just as the words, "So! Tell me *everything*. Does he have a big dick?" came out of her mouth, Michael opened the bathroom door.

"Oh, hey, babe," I said.

"Surely not," he said.

Meredith and I giggled.

"We need to go to a hotel right now," he said.

"No," I said. "I think total immersion is the only way you're ever going to understand me." He closed the bathroom door again. "What you see is what you get, babe!" I yelled after him.

The next day, before we left, my grandmother came over carrying a big pot of her matzo ball soup. God, I love that smell. Savory chicken broth and carrots and celery. Love practically oozed out of that pot, like steam. She put it on the stove and turned to Michael.

"Sit down, I'm going to feed you," she said.

"Oh, no thanks," Michael said, raising a hand in mild southern protest. "I'm not hungry."

"That's okay," she said, as if he had just apologized for offending her. "I'm going to feed you anyway." She put a big bowl in front of him. He looked at it and looked back at me. "What's a matzo ball?" he whispered.

"Just try it," I said. "It's delicious."

He took a nibble and looked totally conflicted, his southern manners clashing with his obvious dislike of this strange Jewish food. "I can't eat this," he whispered, with something like panic in his voice. "I don't eat balls."

I rolled my eyes. "Just eat it," I said. "We're going home in an hour. It's tradition."

At least he could understand tradition.

Finally, much to Michael's obvious relief, we drove back to the airport. He flew back to Birmingham, and I flew back to LA. Before his flight left, I put my arms around his neck. "You did a good job," I said. "I know it wasn't easy."

He smiled. "I guess Alabama isn't so easy for you, either."

"Even Steven," I said, and kissed him good-bye.

After my long flight, I collapsed on the couch in my LA apartment, and almost as soon as my butt hit the cushion the phone rang. It was my mother.

"He's just like your father," she said.

"Not exactly," I said. "Michael is far from a pot-smoking hippie from Brooklyn."

"And he's so much older than you," she said.

"What's thirteen years in the scheme of things?" I said.

"I worry," she said. "He's smart and polite."

"And this is a bad thing?"

"But he's so serious," she insisted. "He doesn't seem to have any sense of humor. He's not one of us. I don't see how this will work."

I think everybody who ever knew Michael and me together wondered how it would work. We really are as different as two people can be, so different that it can seem insurmountable. But I knew we loved each other and I knew we were good for each other. I knew we could fill in for the parts each of us lacked, and make each other whole.

And maybe we would suck at it. And maybe we would be awesome. Or both.

"It's easy to give up," I told my mother. "Getting up every day and trying is what's hard, and valuable. Besides, you and Daddy worked."

"If you say so," she said, doubt in her voice, but no more argument.

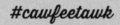

#cawfeetawk

Oftentimes we want to reject what we don't know, but some of life's greatest experiences happen when we step out of our comfort zone and let life happen.

– *Chapter 13* –

"THESE ARE NOT MY PEOPLE"

$\mathcal{M}$ichael and I decided that early August would be good for the move because that would give me enough time to pack up my business and my apartment and my life and get across the continent. I was finally getting used to the idea that my life was going to change, although it was all still theoretical in my mind. Michael and I were getting along so well that I was becoming more and more ready to take the leap.

Michael did all the manly things you would expect. He hired movers, made all the arrangements, and flew out to LA to drive me back "home." But although I was game and kept my chin up and put on a good face and all those clichés of the optimist, part of me was still having a silent and well-hidden panic attack. As I smiled and packed and planned and informed everyone, inside, I kept thinking, *What the fuck did I get myself into? There's so much I haven't done yet with my life.*

It's very hard to decide to cast aside the life you built for yourself, and it's even harder to turn your happiness over to someone else. I have always been an independent person, yet there I was, planning to build a brand-new life around somebody else's already established life. It wasn't like we were both starting something new together and building from the ground up. We were coming together in his world, surrounded by his family, his upbringing, his memories, his culture, his possessions. And I was about to barge in, in all my Jersey glory, and try to make myself at home in the land of debutantes and mint juleps and cucumber sandwiches? I had a hard time even imagining how it would ever work, and I felt lost. How would I find myself again in Alabama? How would I reinvent my life? How would I make my own friends, find my own joy, or be my own person, as Mrs. Michael Sullivan? I didn't want Michael to feel like he had to entertain me all the time, but what was I going to do? I had no job, no purpose, not even any really close friends. No family. Michael was it. *He would be my everything*, at least for a while. It was terrifying—for both of us, even though we didn't talk about it.

And so, we set out, from Los Angeles, Michael cheerful and optimistic, and me, filled with trepidation and anxiety. Michael drove (both literally and figuratively), and as we crossed the city limits out of LA, I looked out the window and mentally said good-bye. I had a sinking feeling that only got deeper and darker as we passed the California state line and headed southeast.

The states that you go through to get from California to Alabama are Arizona, New Mexico, Texas, Louisiana, and Mississippi. To Michael, this was incredibly interesting. He had only flown over or into these states before, and now he was getting to experience that journey to his homeland in a more real way—on the road. We were on the old Route 66, and he told me how historic it was. He wanted to make it into a vacation. Santa Fe was his favorite city, so we took a little detour north from Albuquerque and spent the night there. We checked into a little bed-and-breakfast dripping with southwestern décor, and later took a walk around the pueblos, looking at the art and the people and trying the food.

And as we did this, as I smiled and pretended to be interested, I was thinking, *This is your favorite city? This? Not New York? Not LA? Not even Chicago or Boston or Seattle? Where is Saks? Where is the noise? Where are all the people? And what the heck is adobe?* Then I thought, *How can I marry a guy that likes two-dollar tacos, quiet dusty streets, and houses that look like lumps of clay? How can I marry a guy who reads the whole newspaper cover-to-cover every single morning and actually enjoys it? How can I marry a man who thinks for such a long time before he ever utters a word?*

You can imagine how this line of thought quickly spiraled into despair. My inner monologue got louder with every new city as we got deeper and deeper into the Deep South. As Michael got more cheerful, I got gloomier. At each stop, Michael said something like, "There are so many cool things for us to do here!"

And I always answered with a dubious but hopeful, "There are?"

Frankly, I hadn't seen one interesting thing yet since we left the city limits of Los Angeles. When he dragged me into a restaurant in Texas that awarded a T-shirt to whomever could finish their biggest steak, and Michael didn't even order the steak, I almost lost it. I didn't eat steak, so why would he take me here unless he was at least going to *try* to eat the biggest steak? As I watched him eat the chicken in Texas's most famous steak house, I choked out an idea. "Maybe we could still get married, but I could live in LA and you could live in Alabama?"

He just smiled at me and went back to his chicken. I wanted to stab him with my unused steak knife.

I felt slightly heartened when we drove into New Orleans. The city was bustling with tourists and music, but when we went out for dinner, people were sucking the heads off crawfish, newspapers spread on the tables to catch the carnage. I wanted to die. I couldn't understand what was happening. Here I was, a woman who thought she could fit in anywhere, with anyone, and yet I had never felt so out of place. We held hands as we walked back to the hotel. Later I got into bed and watched Michael brush his teeth. All my senses were turned up, like a superhero's, and I felt ultrasensitive to everything that was happening. I stared at this man who was going to be my husband. I thought, *Do I like the way he brushes his teeth? Do I like boxer shorts? Why are his feet so white?* Everything I hadn't seen when I'd been ring fucking became crystal clear to me, all in an instant. It's all magical when you're working for it, but once it's your reality, the magic can seem to fall away. You start to ask, *What's wrong with him that he wants to spend his life with me?* We had sex that night—vanilla love sex in Louisiana—and I looked around the little hotel room, and I looked at him sleeping and I thought, *This is it. My life is going to be this vanilla. Southern vanilla. Deep southern white-footed vanilla.* Doubts crept in. Serious doubts.

When we drove through Mississippi, I stared bleakly out the window. I couldn't possibly live here. It wasn't home. It was *Deliverance.* I was Hollywood. I was New York. I was *Jersey,* for God's sake. I could blend in anywhere . . . except here. I knew I didn't have the tools to assimilate. You know yourself. Some people can move to a new state and go, "I'm going to do everything I can to fit in here, no matter how weird and foreign it is." Some people move to New York and they can't wait to learn to ride the subway. Other people move to New York and take cabs their entire life because the subway terrifies them. The South terrified me. How could I possibly be happy here? And how could I possibly be a good partner to Michael if I couldn't be happy?

Finally, somewhere in the middle of dinner, in the middle of Mississippi (and in the middle of my fifth glass of wine), I said something. I had to. It was eating me alive and he deserved to know how I was really feeling. I looked around the bar where we were eating and I looked at the people and I said to Michael, "These are not my people. And they know it. They see right through me."

He smiled his infuriating little smile and said nothing.

"I mean it, Michael. This is serious." I could hear my voice starting to rise in pitch and volume. "Do these people know how loud my mother is? I think they do. I think they can actually tell. But do they know what mah-jongg is? I think not. Do they know the words to 'Hava Nagila'? Do they know what beaches make up the Jersey Shore?" I was almost yelling at this point. "Michael! *Do they know what disco fries are?!*"

Again with the smile.

"Michael, listen to me. I mean it. Really listen to me. I've never even been to a Cracker Barrel. I've never eaten in a Waffle House. These are not my people! And now I've given up my career and agreed to live in a world I can't survive in, let alone thrive in. *What have I agreed to here?*"

Michael gave me a long look and took my hand. "Do you love me?"

"Yes!"

"Do you believe that I love you?"

"I do. In fact I believe that nobody will ever love me for exactly who I really am as much as you." It was true. I did believe it. "But I don't think I can do this. I don't think I have it in me."

"You can, and you will, and you're going to be great," he said. "I know it." And that, apparently, was the end of the discussion.

I love him, I told myself. *He loves me.* And I held on to that for dear life.

#cawfeetawk

Fear does not stop failure. It stops success. Never let fear cheat you out of the blessings that are meant for you.

✳ *Part Two* ✳

THE
LONGEST YEAR

It was always so hot, and everyone was so polite,
and everything was all surface but underneath it was like
a bomb waiting to go off. I always felt that way about the South, that
beneath the smiles and southern hospitality and
politeness were a lot of guns and liquor and secrets.

—JAMES MCBRIDE, *THE COLOR OF WATER:*
A BLACK MAN'S TRIBUTE TO HIS WHITE MOTHER

Chapter 14

PLEASANTVILLE

*W*e're all familiar with that uncomfortable banjo tune—the one that makes everyone's asshole immediately clench up. When we drove over the border into Alabama, I couldn't help but hear it in my head. It didn't matter that I'd been here many times before. (Or that *Deliverance* actually takes place in Georgia.) It didn't matter that I'd even worked here. *Living here* was completely different, and it felt like a threat. I saw Alabama in a whole new light and I didn't like it. I was immediately rebellious. Determined to be a foreigner. I was here *under duress!* Even though that was not even remotely true, it was the old scrappy Jaime rearing up and taking over my lizard brain.

But first let's clear up a few misconceptions. The Deep South feels like an alien place to a Yankee, but the Deep South I was about to call home wasn't about banjo playing or moonshine or missing teeth or any of that. This was a different Deep South altogether. I think I might have been able to handle the Honey Boo Boo, trucks-on-cinder-blocks, gun-totin' yahoo Deep South, but instead I found something much more insidious and even more difficult for me to understand: I found Pleasantville.

What the fuck? I'd observed it before, but now I really noticed it. Everyone was so . . . *happy*. Everyone greeted me with a bright smile and a friendly, "How y'all doin' today?" (I still look behind me to see who else they are talking to besides me.) Where was the angst? Where was the dark side? The yelling? The fighting? The flipping of the bird? The road rage? And where were the depressed people wearing black leather and too much makeup? Were those smiles genuine, or were they thin veneers over judgmental sneers? I couldn't be sure. And if they were real, what were they all doing to be so happy? Was it genetic? A product of the incessant sunshine? Were southern people having the best sex ever? And what was wrong with me that I experienced *a whole spectrum* of emotion beyond (a) mild happiness and (b) polite civility?

I was prepared for a South I could grapple with, a South I could yell at about racism and sexism and ignorance. I was ready to take down anybody who got in my face. But nobody was getting in my face! They were all so . . . agreeable! What was I going to do with this place, where fighting was impolite and yelling was unheard of and nobody ever really said what they were actually thinking? I was born to brawl. How was dirty Jersey going to fit into squeaky-clean Alabama, which might be classist and racist and sexist, but I just couldn't be sure because nobody ever said a single rude thing to anybody?

And what about the noise? Where was the noise? The noisy happy raucous confusion I knew from New Jersey, or even LA? I wasn't completely sure whether people in New Jersey turned their car radios up too high and talked too loudly, or whether people in Alabama turned their car radios down too low and talked too softly, but the basic decibel level was radically different. Everyone seemed to clock in within some narrow zone, slightly above "sleeping" and way below "party time!"

I couldn't help wondering what would happen if you took a thousand southern people to Vegas. I'll tell you what would happen: nothing. And I didn't like it. Ala-fucking-bama. Where fun (at least fun the way I always understood it) goes to die.

And now I actually lived there.

At first, I didn't know what to do with myself. I had one year. One year to live in Alabama with Michael before the wedding. One year to plan the wedding. One year to make friends, ingratiate myself to my new family, fit in. One year to *belong*. I felt like I lived beneath the face of a giant clock, ticking down. One year to determine whether I could do it.

I sat alone in that house. That house that belonged to Michael. The house with the microwave in the pantry. *Who keeps a microwave in a pantry?* I had a wedding to plan, and maybe that should have kept me busy enough, but it didn't. Besides, my future mother-in-law had her own thoughts about that.

Now that I was on her turf, Carole was forced on many occasions to introduce me, but she had a disclaimer prepared. "This is Mike's friend from New Jersey." Not fiancée. *Friend.* As if she were warning everyone in the vicinity that she would not be held accountable for whatever I might say or do.

"Michael, if she doesn't stop calling me your friend . . ."

"Babe, let it go," he whispered, patting my arm. "Just give her some time."

Once we started planning the wedding, I wanted to include her. My mother wasn't there, and Carole owned an event flower shop, so I thought maybe this could make her my ally. My first peace offering was to ask her advice.

"Carole, Michael and I want to do engagement photos," I said, thinking she would know a good photographer.

"Oh, that's not necessary."

"Well . . ." I wasn't sure what to say next. What did she mean? I decided to continue on my trajectory. "Put it this way—we are going to do engagement photos and we want to send out engagement announcements."

"Really, Jaime, that's not necessary."

"Who said anything about necessary? It's fun. It's romantic! It's tradition?"

"I have an idea!" Carole said, suddenly brightening. "Why don't you do that in the *New Jersey* newspaper! That would be very interesting for them, I bet!"

What, did she think we have just one newspaper? That everyone in Jersey will be crowding around, reading about me? "Hey, there she is, that one girl who moved to the South!"

"I will do that, Carole. But I want to do it here, too. In my home and in Michael's." I could see her bristling again. Suddenly I realized that she didn't want it to be announced. She was embarrassed. Or perhaps she didn't believe it was really going to happen. Or both.

That's when I had to have a talk with myself. *Okay, Jaime. You have two choices. You can either follow your feelings and continue to get hurt and not like this woman, or you can choose to love her every day, no matter what. And if you continue to love her for who she is, eventually she may learn to love you for who you are.*

I chose the latter. However, it took her a very long time

to love me back. I hadn't earned it yet. She probably saw me as someone who breezed into her world, plucked up her son, and expected to be freely admitted into centuries of southern tradition. She tolerated me, at best. I would go to see her at the flower shop, and she would come to the door and all her girls would be in there working, and she would stick her head out and say, "Hey, what do you need?" It was never, *Come in! So good to see you!* Like entrance to the flower shop required some secret password that I could never hope to be privy to.

Even so, she took over the wedding plans like it was her wedding. I think she was terrified that I might do it all wrong and humiliate her in her own environment. To me, however, this commandeering of my wedding took all the wind out of my sails. Imagine hiring a wedding planner who wants to do everything for you, except she plans the exact opposite wedding from the one you would actually want. I would say things like, "Michael and I want to get married on a Saturday night at seven o'clock, black tie. Friday night will be the rehearsal dinner."

Invariably, she would say, "Why?" and offer some counterpoint. "Just get married on Friday at five PM so people don't have to rent tuxedos."

"Carole," I would counter, "this is the South. Doesn't everybody already own a tuxedo?"

"Well, yes," she would agree, trying to pacify me. "Many do, but not all. And that could become a hindrance. So we'll do it at five."

Everything I said I wanted, everything I chose, she would consider for two seconds, then raise her eyebrows and say, "Hmmmm," which is the southern equivalent of "Fuck no, you are not doing that." Finally, I threw up my hands. "Carole, why don't you just tell me what kind of bourbon I want? Why don't you pick out my dress? Why don't you make up my guest list for me? Why don't you just do it all? Hell, I might as well just get married at the Waffle House."

"Oh, Jaime, don't be ridiculous," she said, brushing me aside with a flick of her perfectly manicured hand. "The Waffle House is for the morning after."

Meanwhile, I spent my days walking around the house or the streets of Birmingham feeling like I was living on the exterior of Michael's life. His neighborhood, his work friends, his monogrammed water cups. I was living in his house, which was now supposedly our house, but was it? It was a bachelor pad, a home that had seen I don't know how many other sets of heels at the door. I was now sleeping in a bed that should have felt warm and inviting, but instead felt cold and used. Some people thought it was romantic. *Oh, it's so romantic, you got engaged and he moved you across the country.* Yeah, and I hung my clothes in his closet, and I slept in a bed that other women had slept in. It was his space and I was trying awkwardly to wedge myself into it and make it my own, but I couldn't.

I could see myself becoming that woman who went to the dry cleaners and wandered aimlessly up and down the aisles of Costco and walked my dog for hours because—what else was there to do? I had already become that woman who stands in the kitchen tapping her fingers, waiting for the clock to strike six, waiting for him to get home from work because he was all I knew and the only person in my world I could really relate to. Honestly, it was my worst nightmare. While I have a sincere appreciation for women who commit to a life in the home because that is what fulfills them and serves them, that is not me. I began to get depressed.

One highlight of my day was the old lady named Jeannie who lived in our neighborhood. She must have been in her late seventies or early eighties, and she had lived in Birmingham her whole life. Whenever I would walk by her house and she was outside, she would pet my cocker spaniel, Jordan, and talk to me.

"How are you liking it, dear?" she would ask.

"It's hard, Jeannie," I would tell her.

Then she would say something profound, like, "Growth, no matter where you plant your roots, is hard. You have to have the perfect mix of sunlight and water and food and even in the best conditions, only the strongest will reach their fullest potential."

"Great. Because I'm starving. I'm dying. I don't think I'm going to make it."

"But just look at you!" she would say. "Every day, here you are, making it."

Sometimes she would try to convince me that the South was a place worth living, and that I should give it a chance. Once, she said, "All the things I love about the South are the things I take for granted. The sunshine, the beautiful flowers, the nice people, the good biscuits, the sweet tea, summer evenings on the porch, and of course the presence of the Lord. Those are the things that I see and hear and feel and live and pray every single day, and have my entire life. They are a part of me."

"I guess that's the problem, Jeannie," I explained. "They aren't a part of me. I have a whole different list of things that I live and pray every single day. This isn't my place. These aren't my people."

"Honey, if we could integrate the schools, we can find a place here for a Yankee," she would say, patting my arm.

One day, she was out in her front lawn pulling weeds when she saw Michael and me together for the first time out on the driveway kissing good-bye as he left for work. I walked over to say hello and she was grinning. "Well, I wanted to believe you moved down here for the hospitality and the sweet tea, but now I've laid eyes on that man and I know exactly why you came. You're going to have to figure out a way to like it, dear!"

"I'll tell you what," I said. "If it doesn't work out, you can have him."

"Honey, I'll take him! Does he like older women?"

"I think he does," I assured her. "In fact, I'm sure of it." And I patted her on the arm right back.

Some days, those were the most fulfilling conversations I had.

Another strange thing I noticed about Birmingham was how invisible I had become. In Jersey, in New York, in LA, people noticed me. I was big and bold and larger than life. But here, for some reason, people didn't see me. They didn't recognize me from high school. They didn't know me from football games. We didn't go to Auburn together. There was nothing recognizable about me, and unlike in other cities, where difference attracted attention, in the South difference repelled it. They didn't know what to make of me, so they pretended I wasn't there. Say all you want about how friendly and nice southern people are. To them, I didn't exist, and it was disconcerting and drained my natural confidence away.

I didn't look like them. I didn't talk like them. And I certainly didn't dress like them. Fashion proved to be a whole different hurdle altogether. One night when I went out with Leigh Anne and some of her friends, I wore a denim stretch one-piece sleeveless jumper with cute booties, big hoop earrings, and red lipstick. It was a very Jersey outfit, I'm not going to lie, but I think I looked hot. I was expecting at least some insults, if nothing else. Instead, when I met up with Leigh Anne, she took one look at me, and all she could say was, "Oh! You look . . . comfortable."

"What do you mean?" I challenged her.

"Um . . . that outfit is very . . . stretchy!" she said, smiling. "It just looks really comfortable."

You know that moment when you realize you wore the exact wrong thing for the occasion? The girl who shows up in the Halloween costume and it isn't a costume party? That's how I felt. Somehow, I got through the night, parading around in public in my crazy Jersey "costume." When I got home I accosted Michael. "Why didn't you tell me this wasn't an appropriate outfit for Alabama?"

"Babe, I didn't realize that was an appropriate outfit for *anywhere*."

"I hate you," I said.

"You know what, babe? It's trial and error. You just gotta get out there and be who you are, and the right people will come to you."

I knew he was right. But it was such a painful lesson to get through that I tried constantly to escape. "Are you sure you want to get married? Maybe we just stay together like Kurt Russell and Goldie Hawn. They seem very happy."

And as usual, Michael would chuckle, knowing that it was my fear. "I'm sure they are very happy," he would simply say.

A couple of weeks later, when I was feeling incredibly lonely, I would say something like, "You don't want to live here *forever*, right? This is like a temporary home. Maybe we'll move up north?"

He was always honest with me. "No," he would say. "This is where I'm going to live and die."

Sometimes I would approach it more blatantly. "Michael, I really don't think I can handle this many life changes at one time. This is the first time since I was seventeen that I am establishing some kind of permanent residency and it's making me extremely uncomfortable." Not only was I giving up everything familiar, but also I was giving up the freedom to run, the freedom to leave. A freedom I had always exercised to survive.

"Come on, I thought you were tough. How does the song go? 'If you can make it there you'll make it anywhere'?"

"That was *New York*," I said. "I could make it *there*."

"Okay, babe. I'll make you a deal." He smiled in a way I can only describe as devious. "If you can find a job in New York or New Jersey that pays as much as I make here, I will entertain the idea."

Challenge accepted. Because *that* was a reason to get a job.

#cawfeetawk

Even if you were the ripest, juiciest peach in the basket, you still won't be right for someone who doesn't like peaches. Kill them with kindness, even if you are doing it through gritted teeth.

Chapter 15

BRITNEY SPEARS AND
THE SWEET TEA EXPERIMENT

I have always defined myself by what I do. My work has always given me a sense of purpose and direction and something to focus on when I didn't know who I was or what I was doing in my personal life. To be without it might have been the worst part of my transition because even though I had a desk in Michael's house and I was writing the occasional celebrity profile or press release for some of my former clients in LA, I didn't really have a job. I didn't feel employed. I couldn't really say, "I'm *this*." And so, I was left without an identity. With a question mark:

"I am . . . ?"

I began to scan the newspapers obsessively for jobs. In the evenings, when Michael came home, I would point out jobs to him, circling them with a red Sharpie like they do in the movies. "Look, a paralegal! I could be a paralegal."

"You could not be a paralegal," he said. "You would be miserable."

"Can you just make some calls? Get me something?"

"You would hate being a paralegal."

"Executive assistant, then," I said, pointing to another ad in the newspaper.

"Jaime. You are not the girl who goes to work at eight thirty in the morning and leaves at five thirty."

"Maybe I am," I argued. "Maybe that's what God's trying to tell me. To go get an office job."

"If that's what you're hearing, I think you're listening to the wrong voice," Michael said, taking the sports section out of my pile of newspapers. "You're listening to the voice of fear, not the voice of fate."

I stopped and stared at him. "That was deep, Michael."

He just smiled. In retrospect, I think he knew there would be no fast fixes for me. He knew who he was marrying, and he knew I would have to go through it. I had to feel every damn twitch of misery before I would ever settle into this life. And he was right. Those were not the jobs for me. I had to find my own way. One day, a friend of a friend mentioned a job opening with a PR firm. *This is it*, I thought.

The firm was in Birmingham and it was sort of edgy and cool. Even though they only did corporate PR, which was completely different from anything I had ever done, I applied. I met with the owner, and she liked the fact that I already had a lot of established national relationships. All the publicists who worked for her only did local PR, and she wanted to see if she could expand nationally. She thought it might work to have me come on board, so I agreed to work for her.

During this time, she was pitching to a local tea company to sign on as a client. This could be my chance to really make my mark, so I went to the pitch meeting.

Now, keep in mind that I am an entertainment publicist. I handle celebrities. This is the world I come from. So we're in this meeting with all these southern tea people, and they're talking about how to expand their visibility. They want to know what I can do for them nationally to garner attention and impact sales. Then it hits me. *I am a genius.*

"I've got it," I say. I used to work with Britney Spears's father, so I know Britney. Britney is from Louisiana. And what do people from Louisiana love? Sweet tea! "We'll ship some of your tea to Britney and then all we have to do is get a photograph of her drinking your tea. One photo will put your tea on the map!"

I waited for the adulation, the applause, the delight. I got some tight, polite smiles. *That's interesting. Hmm, that's a thought,* and somebody changed the subject.

I couldn't understand it. Did these people not see? Were they slow? Surely they would think about it for thirty seconds and realize that this was the key to their nationwide success. I mean, duh . . . we were talking about *Britney*!

After the meeting, the owner of the company called me into her office.

"How do you think it went?" she said.

"Oh, it was great," I said. "It's a lock." Hashtag *nailed it.*

As it turns out, apparently these corporate southern folks didn't find my Britney Spears idea nearly as endearing and smart as I did. In fact, they were, frankly, appalled that Britney Spears could ever be associated with their tea. This was around 2007, and it was true that Britney was having some issues. Apparently, they were offended that this was my contribution, and apparently they also said that maybe I didn't really understand their brand and what they had in mind. I couldn't believe it. Britney would have launched them to a whole new level. And yet I was, and I believe this is how my boss told me they put it, a little too "retro Hollywood" for them.

Seriously? Retro Hollywood? Britney Spears? Who is from Louisiana? My sophisticated and professional response was, "Well, they don't know their asses from their elbows, so good luck trying to get national exposure for their tea. If they think having Louisiana's sweetheart drink their tea is some kind of liability, then they don't know shit about PR."

Maybe being a publicist in Birmingham wasn't going to work out very well for me. I tendered my resignation.

This latest misstep brought me down even farther, and I needed a shot of Jersey. It was time to go home for a while.

I missed Jersey. I missed it with a passion. I missed my family, my friends, and the *Jersey way of things*. It wasn't the first time I'd been back since I had moved to Alabama, and it certainly wouldn't be the last, but it was a visit I needed desperately *at that moment*. Every time I went back to Jersey to visit, I felt this huge weight lifting off me. Finally, I felt comfortable, normal. I fit in again.

"My sister is going through a hard time," I told Michael, carefully assuming an expression of great familial concern.

"What do you mean by a hard time?" he said, not looking away from the newspaper.

"She needs me! Okay? You're not being supportive! Girls are different from boys and you don't understand because you have brothers but my sister needs me!"

He looked at me over his coffee cup. "Okay," he said. He obviously had no intention of arguing with me.

For good measure, I was sure to call Meredith several times during the week when Michael was in the room. "Don't worry!" I said. "I'm coming home. I'll help you through this."

"Through what?" she said.

"I'll be there for you."

"My biggest problem right now is trying to figure out which shade of lipstick to buy at the MAC counter," she said. "I don't really know if that requires you flying home for—"

"Oh my God, Meredith! I will come. Don't worry. This distance won't come between us."

"Okay . . ." she said.

I hung up and eyed Michael. He gave no appearance of listening to me at all. An Oscar-worthy performance, wasted!

That Thursday, I flew to Jersey for the long weekend, and the second I landed on Jersey soil it was like my life in Alabama didn't exist. Meredith picked me up from the airport, and we were sisters together again. We went to the mall. We got our nails done. We ate the food and sang the freestyle music. We went to the shore. We went into the city for a day. I was gulping in everything familiar and I couldn't get enough. People would ask me how it was going in Alabama and I would evade the question with short, clipped answers. I wasn't even all that excited about the wedding planning because I didn't feel like I had control over any of it. I was too busy seeking my future mother-in-law's approval. I missed Michael, but when the weekend was over, I didn't want to go back to Alabama. Yet I told myself it was my duty. I had (mostly) accepted that. But a little break from that duty was fucking awesome.

On Sunday afternoon, Meredith dropped me off at LaGuardia to board the one direct flight back to Birmingham. When I hugged her good-bye, I didn't want to let her go. Because the truth is, I was the one who needed her that weekend, not the other way around, and we both knew it.

At the gate, I noticed a young couple, about my age, with a really cute baby. I commented on how cute their baby was, and ended up seated next to the new mother. The plane was crowded—every seat was full—and we began to chat. They dimmed the lights and she said, "So you're from the North. Where exactly?"

"New Jersey," I said. "How about you?"

"I'm from a little town in Alabama with one stoplight. The most exciting thing in town is the movie theater," she said.

I told her I was getting married and she asked about my fiancé. I told her he was a lobbyist, and one of five boys.

"Wow, that's a lot of boys!" she said.

"It is!" I agreed. "And my future mother-in-law is a florist with a shop in Crestline." We continued to chat, and the talk turned back to weddings, and I mentioned, just randomly, for no real reason except that it was somehow relevant to the context of our conversation . . . that someone I knew had called off his wedding on the actual wedding day. I never mentioned any names. Maybe I mentioned it because I might have entertained the same thought and wanted a genuine southern reaction. I certainly didn't think it was scandalous, just something to consider.

Once we landed, we both said it was nice to meet the other, she gave me her phone number, and she told me to call her if I ever wanted to have coffee. I congratulated her on her baby, and we parted ways. No big deal, right? I got home late that night and went straight to bed.

When *shouldn't* you chat with a stranger on a plane? When you live in Alabama, that's when. Fast-forward to the next day. Michael comes home from work and immediately pours himself a Scotch.

"Starting a little early, aren't you?" I said. Usually if he has a drink, it's much later, after dinner.

"We need to talk," he said.

Uh-oh. For a man who hardly ever utters a word, that is one loaded sentence. I immediately begin to scan my memory for something I might have done wrong. "About what?" I said, trying to sound innocent. Because I was—wasn't I?

"I got a call from my mother today," he said, and gave me a meaningful look.

"Okay . . ." I said. Was this some sort of guessing game?

"Did you tell a plane full of people about someone who called off his wedding the day of the wedding?"

"What? Of course not! Why would I do that?" I said.

"And did you say that you expected southern people to be so warm and friendly until you met my mother, who is as cold as ice?" he said.

I had to admit, this was all starting to sound vaguely familiar.

"I . . . I had a conversation with one person . . . a private conversation on a dark airplane," I stuttered. "I never said anybody's name."

"Did you say your future mother-in-law owned a flower shop in Crestline?" he said. He was turning a disturbing shade of red.

"Maybe . . ." I said.

"And that she had five boys?"

"Okay," I admitted. "But I didn't say it loudly."

"Jaime," he said, as if talking to a child. "You said it in Jersey volume. On a crowded plane. How many florists in Crestline do you think have five boys?"

"But still, how would anyone know who I was talking about?" I said.

"You said it on a plane going to Birmingham on a Sunday night from New York. Who do you think was on that plane, a bunch of businessmen from out of town? Everybody on that plane was from Birmingham, and they all heard you, and my mother got six or seven calls from people, all telling her every word you said."

Shit. You gotta be kidding me? And that's when I knew I wasn't in Jersey anymore.

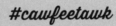

#cawfeetawk

They say the nice part of living in a small town is that when you don't know what you're doing, at least everyone else does.

Chapter 16

THREE PARTIES AND A WEDDING

$\mathcal{B}$etween my engagement and my wedding day, I had three engagement parties/bridal showers: one in Los Angeles, one in New Jersey, and one in Alabama. They could not have been more different, nor could they have more perfectly encompassed the three sides of my personality.

The first party was in Los Angeles, the night before Michael and I left to drive across the country. We held it at a nightclub, and I invited everybody I knew in LA. It was dark and sexy with booming music and we were all dancing and doing shots. Was Michael fazed by the beautiful people, the models, the celebrity friends? Nope, not at all. His steady southern manner and sweet southern charm carried him right through. He was thoroughly present in the experience, never acting like he wanted to be anywhere else. Models would come up to talk to him and I would just stand back and watch, not jealous, just admiring how easily he fit into the environment without changing his behavior at all. It was easy to see why the people who loved me loved Michael. My friends were all frankly a little bit in awe of the man who was supposedly getting Jaime Primak to settle down. They made jokes. A celebrity friend said, "It was nice knowing you. Good luck on the other side of the planet!" A fellow PR person said, "More business for me!" A model told me Michael was yummy, and more than a few of them said some version of, "I cannot *believe* you are doing this!" They weren't criticizing, but they really didn't understand it. Sometimes, I wondered if I did. It wasn't easy to stand on the red carpet, at the peak of my dream career, among so many PR professionals and peers, some of whom I admired and some of whom I envied—this great sense of camaraderie—and know I was walking away from it. But I tried not to get too serious. It was a party! I was there to have fun and kick off my new life! Still, to calm my jangled nerves, I had more than a few shots that night before we hit the road and headed east.

The second party was in New Jersey. It was a big Italian dinner for family and close friends at Federici's, which is my favorite restaurant in Freehold. My whole family came—the Jewish side and the Italian side—and once again Michael did an incredible job of being present. I know it was a lot of "yo" and "oy" for him—funny how you just flip those letters to go from Italian to Jew. When my uncle said to him, "I think my brother would have really loved you and I think you are exactly who he would've chosen for his daughter," we both choked back tears. It was a really important moment for my whole family, and it meant a lot to Michael.

But any party in New Jersey is bound to include some drama. While we were enjoying our meal, shouting over one another, I heard a voice. A familiar voice. *No way*, I thought. Nobody else seemed to hear it. I heard it again. "Jaime?"

Immediately, my body reacted. *Stay calm*, I told myself. *It's probably not him.* "Jaime?" My heart stopped. I turned around. It was my high school boyfriend, in all his Jersey glory, standing behind me. "Heyyyy! Jaime!" he said, opening his arms in a way that seemed both enthusiastic and aggressive. Record scratch! Ripped jean shorts and high tops; he looked like he'd just stepped out of a White Snake video. He looked ridiculous. I glanced at Michael, in his expensive perfectly tailored suit, then looked to Meredith, panicking.

"Anthony! How *are* you!" Meredith said, putting an arm around him and sweeping him away from the table. I saw her across the restaurant, whispering to Anthony.

"Who was that?" Michael said, raising his eyebrows.

Now, I know it's wrong to lie, but the cutoff jean shorts were more than I thought Michael should have to endure. "Oh, just a guy we used to know." Technically, not a lie.

Meredith returned to the table and gave me a *crisis averted* look. I relaxed. As the night went on, a few drinks in, I forgot Anthony was there at all, until I excused myself to go to the bathroom. As I came out of the ladies' room, there he was, pushing me back in. I felt a surge of panic: There was nobody else in the bathroom.

"You're getting married?!" he said. I could smell the Southern Comfort on his breath, but there was nothing comfortable or southern about this situation. I'd been here before. I took a deep breath.

"Yes, I am getting married, and I would hope you would be happy for me."

"Yeah, sure," he sneered. "And does he know what a blood-sucking bitch you are?" Ah, good old Anthony, some things never change.

Before I could answer, there was a knock on the door. "Jaime?" It was Michael.

"Yes. I'll be right out," I said. Michael's voice gave me a surge of courage, as Anthony tried to stare me down. "Move, and don't you dare make a scene," I said. He knew me well enough to know I was serious, so he stepped aside.

I opened the door, and there was Michael. Anthony pushed past me and stopped in front of Michael. He looked him up and down. "I hope your son knows what a blood-sucking bitch he's marrying." I pressed my lips together. I wanted to laugh out loud but I held it in. Michael smiled, looking confused, as Anthony pushed past him. I couldn't decide what was funnier—that guys in Jersey were still wearing cutoff jean shorts, or that Anthony thought Michael was my future father-in-law.

Finally, we had an engagement party in Birmingham, which, as I'm sure you can imagine, resembled my Jersey engagement party in exactly zero ways. Carole wanted to help, which really meant she wanted to take control of the party, and she did. When I said I wanted a taco bar, Carole said we would have it catered. When she asked me how many serving spoons I had (exactly none), she could barely keep from rolling her eyes, and then brought over all her serving spoons. (You would be amazed at how many serving spoons a southern woman can collect. There were fifty people and each could have had their own.) I scanned the guest list, I barely knew a single one. It was a taste of the wedding yet to come.

Our tastes clashed. Everything I wanted, she hated; and everything she wanted, I secretly hated but tried to pretend to like. We never said the word *hate*, of course, but the vast ocean between her sense of what a wedding should be and my sense of what my wedding should be seemed impossible to navigate. Still, I would not go down without a fight; I would love her, damn it, even if it killed me.

The truth is, much of it was my fault. I was giving my future mother-in-law so much power by constantly seeking her approval. That right there is a recipe for disaster. No relationship can flourish with that form of imbalance. She took over because she thought somebody had to make sure the wedding wasn't a complete embarrassment, but also because I let her. Whenever the subject of the wedding came up, I felt as though Carole determined my worth, and this was damaging to my self-confidence and made me feel completely alone. I was chasing the approval of somebody who wasn't ready to give it to me yet. I think in her mind, agreeing with any of my wedding choices meant she approved of me, and at that time she just didn't. Truth is, she didn't know what to make of me, so she kept me at a distance. Ultimately, this is one of the surprising lessons I've learned from her: You don't have to let everybody in. It's okay to be polite and keep a person at arm's length until you're certain you're prepared to embrace them.

Occasionally, I talked to my family in Jersey about the wedding plans, and I think everyone was generally happy for me, but it's a lot easier to get excited about a wedding when you're right there helping with the planning. When you're in another state, connected by phone or text, you're not really in it. As a result, my wedding was completely bereft of Jersey. It was an Alabama wedding, whether I liked it or not. When people from Jersey asked me, *How's it going with your mother-in-law?* or *How's it going with Michael?* I would simply say, *I don't want to talk about it.* Because what was there to talk about? It wasn't terrible. I wasn't miserable. And in some ways, without my dad there, I felt like my wedding would be missing something very important anyway, so I was less invested in the act of marrying Michael than I was invested in the idea of actually being married to him.

But there was much work to be done before we could begin our marriage. I wanted a sit-down dinner. Carole said that was unheard of and we would have a buffet. I wanted a DJ who would blast '80s music all night long so my friends and family could dance until the sun came up. Carole envisioned a tasteful event with a small band; a party where guests would show up, have one drink, a little food, and go home. No pressure or expectation to stay too long.

I had to keep reminding myself that in the South, girls tend to get engaged a lot younger than in the North, and when they do, it's a family affair. Generations go together to shop for dresses. The mother-in-law, the grandmother-in-law, the grandmother, mother, sisters, bridesmaids. They're drinking champagne and hanging out at bridal shops for five hours. I had none of that. Nobody was offering me champagne. One weekend when I went back to Jersey, my mother and I went to David's Bridal on Route 9 in Freehold and looked around halfheartedly until my mother said, "Oh, just pick one." I was never the girl who dreamed about my wedding dress, the perfect ring, and the romantic proposal. I like to think I was smart enough at the time to know that love wasn't enough to make a marriage. I wasn't that girl scribbling MRS. MICHAEL SULLIVAN all over the cover of my Trapper Keeper (though I do love a Trapper Keeper). I wasn't swept up in the romance. Maybe I lost out, but honestly, I felt like I wanted the marriage. I didn't need the wedding to confirm my feelings, I just wanted it to be over so I could get on with my life and figure out who Mrs. Michael Sullivan actually was.

But I was also worried about Michael's passivity during the whole wedding tug-of-war. Carole and I disagreed about every detail, but Michael didn't seem to care about the details. He was flatly agreeable, never got in the middle, and it made me insecure. Was there more going on here, a larger reason why he didn't want to make a big deal out of the wedding? I started to have horrible visions of Michael doing what Big did on *Sex and the City*, when the wedding was all just too much and he felt disconnected and never showed up. Would Michael leave me at the altar? The thought chilled me to the bone.

But Michael held steady. Carole and I each made some concessions. The wedding would be held at seven o'clock on Saturday night, with the rehearsal dinner the night before, *but* it would be at the country club. We would have a DJ, *but* we would have a buffet. We managed to form an uneasy truce, and the wedding date grew nearer and nearer. We were two months away. Then one month. Then three weeks. And then, something unthinkable (at least to my mother-in-law) happened. To us. But at first, just to me.

#cawfeetawk

All healthy relationships take work. None of them, romantic or otherwise, come and stay easy. But the best of them are when someone shows up, puts in the work, and stays even when it's easier to walk away. Truth is, I wanted Carole's approval because I knew deep down she would one day be my greatest ally. And she is. So don't give up. The relationship you're working toward is just at the end of the buffet line.

Chapter 17

SNOT ROCKETS FIRED
IN THE GOVERNOR'S MANSION

I found out six days before the wedding. But let's rewind two weeks earlier because that's when I had my first clue.

On May 5, I went to the governor's mansion for an event with a friend—a weird luncheon with a bunch of women wearing hats that looked like satellites. You could probably see them from space. I was sitting there, conspicuously bareheaded, having my lunch of watercress and cucumber tea sandwiches or whatever the hell they were serving, and suddenly I had the strange feeling that I had wet my pants.

I excused myself to go to the bathroom, and there it was, sitting, quivering, in my underwear: a snot rocket the size of a giant roach. Ew. It was big and thick and I thought I was becoming an X-Man. I was turning to jelly from the inside out. It was frankly disgusting, but I dealt with it in the way a woman must, and I went back to the table, feeling slightly grossed out. I whispered to my friend, "Oh my God, a snot rocket just shot out of my crotch. I've never seen anything like it."

She gave me a quick stern look—a look I was getting used to seeing, that I knew implied, *We don't say things like that out loud, especially not at the governor's mansion!* But I think she took pity on me because she leaned in very close and in a whisper that was barely audible, she said, "That's a good sign, actually. It means you're ovulating."

Whoa whoa whoa, wait a minute. I had been on birth control for fifteen years. *Fifteen years.* My gynecologist told me that it could take a few months for my fertility to be restored after going off birth control, so we decided together that since the wedding was on May 26, I could go off the patch at the end of March. And Michael and I had just . . .

"Oh shit," I hissed back to her in my Jersey-volume whisper. "Michael and I had sex this morning!" Several of the large hats turned in my direction.

My friend leaned in closer. "Did he, like . . ."

"What?"

"Like, you know . . ." She made some random hand movement.

"What? Did he what?" What could she *mean*?

"You know . . . did he . . . *finish*?"

"Oh! You mean like, did he *come*?"

Her eyes darted around and she put her finger to her lips. I kept forgetting how well my Jersey whisper carries around these decibel-challenged southerners.

"*Inside you?*" she said, her voice barely audible.

"Well, yeah," I said. "But I thought I wasn't fertile—my doctor said they've been suppressing my ovulation for so long that it would take a while to get going again."

"Well. I'm sure it's fine," she said, with that southern way of making everything seem all right. She patted my arm. "What are the chances that you'll get pregnant the first time you have sex after being on birth control for fifteen years?" She reached for her mint julep, and I knew the conversation was over.

But holy shit. I couldn't stop thinking about it, now that she had put the idea in my head that Michael might have put something (someone?) in my uterus. After lunch, I got up to stroll around the grounds, as people do at these things, and while I maintained what I thought was an admirably calm exterior, my inner dialogue was raging. *I'm definitely knocked up. There is no question. This is exactly what would happen to me. I would find the best possible way to offend my future southern family. So what am I going to do? Do I tell anybody?*

I calculated. Could I get away with supposedly getting knocked up on my wedding night? How close were we? How pregnant was I? *Oh my God, how pregnant was I?* A man offered me a mimosa and I just glared at him. *How dare he try to poison my baby! Doesn't he realize I'm a pregnant woman?* Just minutes ago I had been in the bathroom mopping up a snot rocket and now I was a ferocious mama bear protecting my unborn child from the ravages of fetal alcohol syndrome.

Even though I probably wasn't pregnant at all. Because how could I be?

That night, back home, I couldn't stop thinking about it all, so I decided to tell Michael. "Let me tell you what happened to me today," I said. I went into all the gory details, of course.

"Ewww," he said.

"I know, right? It was totally gross. It wasn't liquid, it was actually solid, like you could pick it up with your hands and hang pictures on the wall with it."

"I'm forty-four years old and this is the most disgusting conversation I've ever had," he said.

"My friend said it means I'm fertile," I said, testing the waters. "She said it means that's the time you get pregnant. And we . . ." I stopped, letting the rest sink in. I looked at him meaningfully. But he just shrugged.

"Well, obviously that can't happen because we're not married yet," he said.

"Um, Michael, I don't think my uterus knows we're not married. Maybe your sperm know, so they'll just swim right past my egg like well-behaved gentlemen?"

He gave me a look, but it wasn't a worried look, so I decided not to worry, either. At least, not too much.

Fast-forward two weeks to May 21, the week before the wedding. I was at the Regions Charity Classic, a golf tournament in town. Michael was away on a bachelor golf weekend with his brothers and I was hanging out with my only Yankee friend, Michael Choy. We were walking around outside, and my stomach was killing me. I felt gassy and bloated and I figured I was getting my period and the whole snot rocket thing could soon be written off as a near-miss. Or maybe I was just nervous about the wedding. Pre-wedding gas? Or maybe it was a combination. Oh God. My period during my wedding? That would be just my luck.

My friend Michael Choy, or Choy as I refer to him, is from Jamaica, Queens, so he is about as mouthy and inappropriate as I am. I hang out with him whenever I'm about to crack from trying too hard to behave myself. Fortunately for everyone, we were outside, so the, um, shall we say *fallout* from my gassiness was at least dissipating in the outdoor air. But not enough to escape the notice of Choy.

"Dude!" he said. "Is that *you*? I have to know because you are walking in front of me. And if it's not you, this golf course smells like shit."

"Don't make fun of me!" I said. "I don't know what's wrong with me. My stomach hurts so bad. I think it's my nerves."

"If you're so nervous about this wedding that you produce *that* smell, you definitely shouldn't be getting married," he said, wrinkling his nose.

"Oh my God, this is awful," I said. "Maybe I need a soda or something."

"Or *something*," he said. "Like a butt plug."

We went into a VIP tent to look for something carbonated, and they were serving hot dogs, and all of a sudden the scent of those hot dogs hit me. "I can't smell this!" I said. "Get me out of this fucking tent!"

"Smell what?" he said.

"Are you *kidding me*? It's like somebody shoved two hot dogs into my nostrils! I've got to get out of here!"

"What is wrong with you?" he said, following me out but trying not to walk directly behind me. "You're farty and smelly and haven't stopped complaining."

I started crying. "Stop picking on me!" I wailed.

"And crying? Oh my God. Why are you so sensitive? You must be getting your period."

"I'm nervous about the wedding!" I repeated. "Let's go to Walgreens. I need Pepto-Bismol."

"Agreed," he said.

We left the charity event and drove to Walgreen's. As I walked through the store, trying my best to keep from crop dusting everyone in aisle seven, I found the Pepto. I picked up the pink bottle and read the label: *Do not use if you are pregnant or nursing*.

Shit. What if . . . what if . . . I knew I couldn't be pregnant. Because Michael said I couldn't. Because we weren't married. But I felt so *not myself* that I decided to meander casually over to the pregnancy aisle.

"What are you doing?" said Choy.

I didn't answer. I was too busy looking at all the tests. Which one was the best? Which one was the most accurate? On a sudden impulse, I picked one of each.

"Oh my God," mumbled Choy. "You have got to be kidding me."

We went to the register and I dropped the armful of pregnancy tests on the counter. They came to over two hundred dollars, but I didn't care. If even one of those tests was negative, I would know I wasn't pregnant. I paid. "Take me home," I said.

"Gladly," said Choy.

He dropped me off, and finally I was home alone. I opened all the tests. I laid them all out on the edge of the bathtub, and one by one, I peed on every single one. And then I watched. Smiley faces. Plus signs. And most threatening of all, digital results in plain English: YES and PREGNANT and CONGRATULATIONS, YOU ARE ABOUT TO HAVE A SHOTGUN WEDDING.

No. No no no. But wait—maybe a smiley face meant, "Phew! You're not pregnant! Yay!" Maybe a plus sign was like a thumbs-up for dodging a pre-wedding bullet. Maybe they were all negative! I checked every box, every instruction leaflet. Positive. Positive. Positive. Pregnant. Pregnant. Pregnant.

I threw up my hands. "Obviously these are all wrong," I said out loud to the toilet. "Obviously, because I am not pregnant the week before my wedding. Obviously. I'll have to get some more tests that are more accurate. But I'll call Dr. Huggins first. I'll ask his opinion about what brand to get, so I don't waste any more money." Dr. Huggins was and is my ob-gyn. His office would be closed on a Sunday, but I would leave a message.

"Dr. Huggins, this is Jaime Primak. It's urgent that you call me right away!"

Ten minutes later, the phone rang.

"What's going on?" he said.

"Okay, here's the situation," I said. "I need your professional opinion. I bought these pregnancy tests." I listed all the brands. First Response, Clearblue Easy, Generic, You're Certainly Knocked Up or Not Knocked Up. I asked, in his professional opinion, which is most accurate.

He cleared his throat. "They are all pretty accurate," he said. "Why?"

"Well, that's not possible because they are all telling me the same thing, and that can't be accurate."

"Really," he said. "And what are they telling you?"

"They all say I'm . . . pregnant," I said, choking out the last word. "So they must be wrong, because I'm getting married in one week, and I'm wondering which test I can get that will give me an accurate answer."

"How many pregnancy tests did you take?" he said.

"Nine."

He sighed. "You took nine pregnancy tests, and they all say you are pregnant?"

"Yes! This is what I'm saying!" Jersey loud now.

"Then congratulations, Jaime. You're pregnant."

"What?" I said, horrified. "And you call yourself a doctor? You don't know I'm pregnant. You haven't even seen me! You haven't even examined me or done a blood test or anything! How can you make such a hasty assertion, based on some urine I peed out after drinking seven Gatorades?" I was clearly in denial.

"If your urine was that diluted and it was in the middle of the afternoon, your HCG levels would be—"

"Hold on, don't start in with the medical jargon. Let's focus on what we're really talking about," I said, feeling frantic. "Let's focus on how I am *not pregnant one week before my wedding*."

Now, keep in mind that Dr. H knows me and loves me and he knows what a conversation with me involves. He is very patient but has the annoying habit of sticking to the facts. "You're definitely pregnant," he said.

"Listen," I said. "I would really appreciate it if you didn't speak in such absolutes. I think you need to examine me first, and do a blood test. Then and only then will I listen to anything so definitive. Until then, this is all just crazy talk."

"If it will make you feel better, come to my office tomorrow at eight thirty AM and we will do the blood test."

"Okay!" I said. "Thank you! Now we have a plan in place. A plan to *investigate* this situation. A plan that we have to execute before you start throwing around imprudent phrases like *You're definitely pregnant*."

"Okay, Jaime. But in the meantime, I'm going to ask that you don't take any aspirin, don't drink any alcohol, and don't . . ."

"Already with the rules!" I cried. I had a sudden disturbing thought. "Should I tell Michael?" I asked him.

"I feel one hundred percent confident that you are pregnant. Whether the baby will take or not, whether you'll still be pregnant in six weeks or not, that I can't say. But *today*? You're pregnant, so tell Michael if you want to."

"Well, that remains to be seen," I said. "But okay." I hung up the phone and sat there for a minute, my brain vibrating. Finally, I asked nobody in particular, "What am I going to do now?"

The line of plastic sticks and positive signs on the edge of the tub had nothing else to offer. So what else could I do but go back to Walgreens? I was supposed to pick up Michael from the airport in five hours so I felt like I needed to get just a little more proof before I dragged him into this *probably imaginary* drama.

I felt like the digital test was the bossiest one because it actually said the word PREGNANT. So I picked up another digital test. Then two. Because why not be sure?

I went back home and peed on both tests, and they both came up with that word: PREGNANT. The P-word. "You bitches," I said to the insolent plastic sticks.

But just in case, on the weird unlikely off-chance that the word could be true, I wrapped one of the tests up in some colored tissue, like a gift. I took out my little pocket video camera and set it up in the bedroom so it was ready to record.

When I saw Michael at the airport, I almost cried from a wave of emotion, but I swallowed it back. I smiled and asked how his trip went. He told me all about it, but I could barely focus. Golf golf golf, snooze snooze snooze. We got home and I followed him into our bedroom and watched him as he started to unpack.

Then I slyly turned on the video camera I had set up and said, "Michael, honey, I have a present for you. Come stand right here."

He paused, looking suspicious, but he came over next to me. "What?" he said.

I handed him the tissue-wrapped digital test. He opened it, and said, "Oh. That's nice. Thank you," and he stuck it in his pocket.

"Uh, what are you doing?" I said. "There's pee on that."

"What?" he said. "Pee? On a pen?"

"A pen? Oh my God. No, Michael. It's *not* a pen. Take it back out of your pocket, please, and look at it."

He took it back out and looked at it. He opened the top. "What is this?" he said, closing it back up.

"Open it and read what it says," I said slowly, like I was talking to a preschooler.

He sighed and took out his reading glasses. I was getting exasperated. He looked at it for a long minute.

"It says *pregnant*," he finally said.

"Congratulations," I said.

"Whose pregnancy test is this?" he said, peering over the top of his glasses at me.

Now it was my turn to give him the sarcastic look. "It's the neighbor's. Surprise! Our neighbor is pregnant! How fun for us!"

"What?"

"Michael! Get a clue! Snap out of your southern denial! This is *my* pregnancy test. This is *our pregnancy test*! Maybe it's wrong, but Dr. Huggins thinks it's right. He says I'm pregnant, but I'm going to confirm tomorrow. So maybe it's wrong. But it's probably true. I'm probably pregnant."

"I don't get it," he said.

"Yeah, I don't really get it, either, but according to this and about five hundred other pregnancy tests, that's the deal."

After an intentional pause, he sighed. "How did this happen?"

Not the comforting reaction I was secretly hoping for. "Gee, Michael. I don't know, but if I had to guess, I would blame that snot rocket in my underwear that day we had sex, and also your sperm that apparently did not understand our current premarital status. And *this* is what happened."

"Oh," he said. "Okay." He looked at me again and I couldn't read his expression at all. "I really need to unpack." He handed the pregnancy test back to me and left me sitting there on our bed staring at the P-word.

After a minute, I jumped up and followed him into the closet. "Oh no. I don't think so. You don't get to just walk away from this. What exactly do you mean when you say *I need to unpack*? Is that a good *I need to unpack* or a bad *I need to unpack* or a total-denial *I need to unpack*?" I said, waving the pregnancy test in the air for emphasis.

"I'm not sure," he said, not looking at me. "Maybe that third one."

"Michael, are you seriously telling me that you're not happy about this? While I'm still having a hard time believing this, if there *is* a baby, you'd better be damn ecstatic about it!"

He didn't answer. I stormed out and went into the kitchen to pout and eat Doritos, which suddenly tasted delicious. We didn't discuss it again. I barely slept that night.

The next morning I went to see Dr. Huggins, and the nurse gave me the blood test. I went home and at about one PM, the nurse called me.

"Based on your levels, I would guess you're about four weeks along," she said. "I'd like you to come back in on Wednesday to make sure the levels are going up." This was Monday. My wedding was on Saturday.

I called Michael. "You'll be delighted to know that Dr. Huggins just called me, and I really am actually pregnant. And by the way, I videotaped your little *I need to unpack* nonsense, and when this baby is born, and is at an age to understand what a dipshit you are, I'm going to show him or her that video. And then he or she will know exactly who loves him or her more." Admittedly, I was feeling a little vengeful. And hormonal.

"I never said . . . I just . . . I don't know. I need to go." And he hung up. That motherfucker. I had every premeditated intention of hanging up on *him*.

I realized he wasn't ready to talk about it, so . . . we didn't talk about it. It wasn't going to change the result, but I realized that until the wedding was over, in Michael's mind this was going to have to be the thing that wasn't happening. I rubbed my belly. "Maybe it will be just you and me, kid," I said softly. "But I'll always be here for you. I've got your back." That's the moment I fell in love with the baby I now knew existed. I wanted it. It had to work. I needed it.

Then my mind suddenly registered the last thing the nurse

had said about these so-called levels and what they might reveal at my next appointment. Now that I was sure of the baby and sure I was madly in love with the baby, I was terrified that there may no longer be a baby. And hadn't he said something about not knowing whether the baby would still be there later? What did *that* mean? I spent the next few days walking around like I was made of glass.

On Wednesday, I went back to Dr. Huggins. The nurse took more blood. I was practically hysterical at this point, having gotten myself completely worked up about what might happen. What if it was over after it had barely begun? Now that I was pregnant with *an actual person*, I wanted to know and love and protect this person. A thing was happening in my body, and I had a job to do: I had to be sure those numbers went up. I had ownership. It was my little Tic Tac in there, and the numbers *would go up*, if for no other reason than the sheer force of my will.

After they took the blood, I sat there.

"You can go," said the nurse.

"Well, I'm just going to wait here for the numbers," I said.

"It will be hours," she said.

"Oh. All right . . ." I stood up and Dr. Huggins walked in the room. He must have noticed my look of despair and resolve. He hugged me. "The numbers are going to go up," he said. "You're healthy, you're young, and there is nothing that would lead me to believe anything would happen otherwise."

I took a deep breath and went home.

I spent those hours sitting in a chair, my hand on my belly, praying to God that I could keep this baby. When my phone rang, I looked at the number and I got this sick feeling. *God, please, please, please, let the numbers go up.*

"Hello!" I said enthusiastically. The numbers would go up due to my optimism!

"Jaime, it's Dr. Huggins." *Oh crap. He's calling me personally. He's calling to tell me there is something wrong with my baby.* "The numbers were four twenty-eight on Monday and now they're eight sixty . . ." I couldn't even hear the numbers. I just wanted the verdict. "So it looks like your body is doing exactly what it's supposed to be doing. Go get married this weekend and have a great time, and we'll touch base next week."

I cleared my throat. Was I hearing correctly? "Just to be sure. Just to clarify, I'm still pregnant and everything is okay so far, right?" I wanted the answer in plain English.

"Oh dear God," he said. "Yes. You are pregnant. Anything I tell you from this point forward will always refer back to the fact that you are indeed pregnant. So you don't need to ask me that anymore."

"Got it!" I said trying to sound convinced. It would not be the last time I questioned the reality of my pregnancy, and I didn't yet realize that this is a thing we women do. Pregnancy feels like such an improbable miracle that it is easy to doubt it, even when all the evidence points to the simple facts. Because you can't *see* the baby yet. You can't *feel* the baby yet. Believing in it feels like an act of faith, and I was a doubting Thomas.

I hung up the phone and I took a walk around a little shopping area in Crestline, and everyone was smiling and going about their business, but all I could think was, *I'm pregnant. Do these people notice? Can they tell? Am I just a random woman order-*

ing frozen yogurt, or can everyone clearly see that I'm a pregnant woman ordering frozen yogurt? Are they smiling at me because they are polite southerners, or are they smiling at me because they know I am a mother-to-be? I caught my reflection in a shop window. *Do I look pregnant? Am I getting fatter? Will my wedding dress still fit? What does this mean? Can I have sex on my wedding night? I can't drink alcohol. But I ordered the fish! Can I eat the fish? Oh my God, what are the rules?* I had so many questions, but I didn't dare bother Dr. Huggins. The wedding, just three days away, suddenly seemed like some random thing I had to do, hardly the most important part of my week. *This* was the most important part of my week. The most important part of my *life*. And my mother was flying in on Thursday. She'd had lots of babies. I could ask her *everything*. She was going to *die* of joy. Just like I felt I would.

#cawfeetawk

As much as we want to plan every detail of our life, the universe has a way of surprising us with unexpected things—things that have the potential to make us happier than we ever originally planned.

Chapter 18

SECRETS, LIES, AND LUCK

*M*y mother was coming for the wedding. I was pregnant. The only time Michael and I had discussed the pregnancy again was when he asked me not to tell *anybody* until after the wedding, and I agreed. So I couldn't tell anyone. It would be a huge scandal in Michael's family. And yet, the one person I had already told hadn't given me any kind of satisfactory reaction: Michael.

Clearly, I was going to have to tell my mother.

I would buy a new pregnancy test and pee on it and give it to her. I silently cursed the pregnancy test industry for making tests that only last one hour. (By the way, that is so *annoying*! If you're going to charge me twenty bucks for a pregnancy test that says the word PREGNANT, can the word last more than an hour?)

I bought yet another test, and peed on it right before I left to pick my mom up from the airport. When we got home, and she got out of the car, I said, as casually as I could, "Listen, I think Daddy sent me a gift for my wedding." She looked at me like I had clearly gone off the deep end. "Here," I said, handing her the pregnancy test.

"Is this a pen?" she said.

"Oh my God!" I said. "No! What is it with the pen? Is this a generational thing? Read it!"

"I can't see without my glasses," she said.

"Oh for God's sake. You're ruining it!" I said. "Everybody is ruining it!"

She squinted at it in the sunlight, then she looked up at me.

"It says *pregnant*," she said.

"Congratulations," I said. "You're going to be a grandma again."

She let out a giant Jersey sob of joy. She fell to her knees in the grass. She looked up at me beatifically, tears streaming down her cheeks. "Oh, Jaime! Is it true? Could it really be true? It's everything I've dreamed about for you!"

"Now, *that's* what I'm talking about!" I announced to the general area.

And it was. She was over the moon. But I began to doubt my decision to let her in on a secret as soon as she stood up and got that *Who are we going to tell next?* look in her eyes. This was going to require some damage control. "Now, look, Ma. We can't tell anyone. *Not anyone!*" My mother-in-law absolutely could not know about this. My being pregnant before the wedding would be the scandal of the century in her world.

"All right. Got it!" she said, conspiratorially. "It's our secret. It's our *thing*."

"No, Mom. It's not a *thing*. We're not on a mission. It's not a joint venture. I'm pregnant, and I'm just letting you know, but this is private and a little bit inappropriate so you are *not going to tell anybody before the wedding*. It's that simple."

"Right!" she said gleefully, and winked at me. I was going to regret this.

"Stop winking, Ma. This is not a game. I'm serious. Just forget I told you."

"I am forgetting this instant!" she said, and winked at me again.

"Ma. You're winking, which tells me that you are *not* forgetting. Nobody can know that you know. Not even Michael. *Do you understand?*"

"Got it!" she said, obviously thrilled beyond all description that I had let her in on the secret. Her face twitched as she suppressed another wink.

We went back to the house to get her settled in, and when Michael got home, my mother immediately jumped up from the couch. "Hiiiiiiiii," she said, drawing out the word, looking at him sideways, and batting her eyelashes.

"Hi . . . ?" he said, raising his eyebrows.

"Hi . . . *Daddy!*"

Now it was my turn to jump up from the couch. "Oh my God, Ma! Really? What did we *just* talk about?"

Michael looked annoyed. "I thought we agreed we weren't telling anybody."

I sighed. "Well, it's my mom, and moms don't count, and frankly, your reaction sucked. *She* fell in the grass and cried."

"Great. Well, now you told somebody. I hope that's not bad luck." He shrugged and walked away.

That man knows me way too well. It was his not-so-subtle way of punishing me.

"What? What did you say?" I said, chasing after him. "Bad luck? What do you mean? Are you trying to tell me that telling my mother could make something bad happen?"

"We agreed not to tell. And you broke the agreement. It was a sacred agreement."

"Michael Sullivan, don't say things like that. That's a horrible thing to do. There is nothing *sacred* about your refusal to tell your uptight family, and you shouldn't even *say* the words *bad luck* around me!" I made the sound of spitting three times. "Pew, pew, pew!" (It's a Jewish thing.)

He shrugged again, went into his office, and closed the door.

"Ma! Did you hear that? How do I take the bad luck off my baby?"

My mother looked horrified and began to wail. "Oh my God! Jaime, what have you done? What have you done to my *grandbaby*?"

Michael came out of the office. "See what you did?" I said, pointing at my mom, then putting my arm around her to comfort her.

"Hey, this is on you," he said, and went to pour himself a Scotch.

#cawfeetawk

Once it leaves your lips, it's no longer a secret.

Chapter 19

AGAINST ALL ODDS

$\mathcal{F}$inally, it was Friday—the day before the wedding, and the day of the rehearsal dinner. All morning, people came into town—my sisters, my brother, my friends. With each new arrival, my mom kept giving me that look—that sly smile, those raised eyebrows, that elbow in the ribs.

"Stop it!" I hissed under my breath. "Stop it! You are calling attention to the whole thing!" She would just gaze fondly at my abdomen. "Ma, I swear, if you do anything to even *suggest* the *idea* of pregnancy when my mother-in-law is in the room, you are dead. *Dead!*"

"Jaime!" she protested. "I would *NEH-vah*! I would *NEH-vah* do that!" But the second Michael brought his mother into the house, my mother sidled up to her like a con man with stolen watches inside his trench coat and said, out of the side of her mouth, "So, Carole . . . what do you think about us having *grandbabies* togethah?"

Is she fucking kidding me right now?

Of course, Carole innocently believed it was all theoretical. "Well, I think at the appropriate time it might be nice," she said.

I shot my mom a vicious look. She pretended not to see. "Well, who's to say what appropriate is anyway?" she said. "Appropriate's relative, don't you think, Carole?"

This is happening right now, I thought. Michael whispered to me, "I want to die. Right now, I want to die."

"I'm right behind you," I whispered back.

But then, without another word, my mother sallied away gaily, obviously pleased with herself for giving us mutual heart attacks the day before our wedding, without giving anything away to anybody. Miracle of miracles.

Later that day, we rehearsed the wedding, mapping out the steps, but I barely remember it. Afterward, we went to meet all our friends and family for the rehearsal dinner at the hotel where Michael would stay that night, and where we would both stay after the wedding. As we came in one by one and found our seats, the outside patio overlooking the golf course was filled with warmth and laughter, and I felt so happy to be there.

Granted, there was culture clash. My family and friends were loud, brash, and ate like there was no tomorrow, while Michael's family members were quiet, subdued, and a little bit startled by the noise coming from the Jersey side. At one point my uncle, my father's brother, came up to Michael and me. "This is really a Christian thing, huh? Will there be a rabbi tomorrow?"

Michael smiled uncomfortably. "No, Phil. No rabbi. Jaime is Catholic now."

My uncle shook his head. "Okay, but it's bad luck not to have a rabbi. It's your wedding, though. Do what you want." He shook Michael's hand and headed back to the dessert table.

Michael shot me a look. "He only knows one way. This will be good for him," I said. Sure, we were a hodgepodge of religion and region, but I didn't mind. I looked out at everyone, Michael at my side, and in that moment I loved them all. Instinctively, I put my hand over my belly, bringing my unborn child into the potpourri of people who were soon to be combined into one family, like it or not.

After dinner, we all made our way to the outside bar for a drink. (Except me. I was "fake" drinking, which is much harder than it looks.) It was a beautiful evening with a slight breeze and the view was gorgeous, the moon shining over the rolling green of the golf course. Everyone was milling around visiting. I was talking to a group of my Jersey friends when I heard clinking. I looked up to see Michael standing on a chair.

I knew the groom was supposed to make a speech at the rehearsal dinner, but because Michael is a man of few words and hidden emotions, I didn't expect that he would hold with this tradition. I didn't think he was that guy. I was wrong. Something had changed in him, and it wasn't just the few drinks he'd had. He was about to be a married man.

I looked at him and realized all over again how incredibly sexy he was. He had a whiskey in one hand and a cigar in the other, and looked happier than I had ever seen him. He called out, "I don't know where my bride is!"

"Here she is!" someone yelled, pointing at me.

Everyone was turning to look and pointing to me. People began to shuffle and nudge me forward. He spotted me in the crowd, and as soon as I was standing in front of him, looking up, he began an honest-to-goodness speech. I looked around for note cards. Had he written this down? Had he memorized it? I gazed up at him in awe.

"Jaime and I would like to thank everybody for coming," he said. "Especially those of you who traveled from out of town." He cleared his throat, and everyone fell silent. "If someone had told me that as a man, I would someday find myself broken, I would never have believed them. But things happen in life, and sure enough, I was a broken man. When that happened, if someone had told me that it would be a woman who put me back together, I never would have believed that, either."

A collective "Awwww."

"I'm not a man of many words and I'm not a man with much sentiment, but I don't want to marry this woman tomorrow without saying tonight that she is exactly what I prayed for. She is everything that I need to be whole. And as cliché as it sounds, she really does make me a better man. I wish her father could be here." My mother took my hand, and my sisters pulled in close. We choked back tears. "I know he would be incredibly proud of the woman she is today. Jaime, please come up here with me."

He stepped off his chair and held out his hand. I stepped forward and took it. He said to me, "I'm going to do something now that I'll do once tomorrow and probably never again. I'm going to kiss you in front of all these people." I smiled at him, truly, purely happy in that moment, and he gave me a big kiss, bending me backward into a little dip. It was a good one, a million miles away from that first awkward kiss we had both suffered through just months before. I felt dizzy. Everybody clapped and Michael raised his glass. "A toast to my beautiful bride!"

I was holding a drink, and when Michael raised his glass, everyone began to clap and I moved the glass toward my mouth, ready to take just one sip, which surely wouldn't hurt anything.

"Just do it for pretend!" my mother bellowed from across the room.

Oh. My. God. Luckily, the whole room was cheering and drinking and talking and judging one another, and those who did hear her looked at her like she was the lunatic. Thank God for small favors. She leered at me, her grin irrepressible. I glared at her. She raised her hands in a helpless gesture, then pointed her finger at me from across the room and called out, "Enough with the faces, Jaime! Be happy!"

And I was.

My future father-in-law, Dave, came over to shake Michael's hand, and I leaned over. "Hey, Papa Dave, I dare you to kiss Carole in front of everyone."

He laughed and shook my hand, too. "I accept your dare!" he said. He walked right over to her, put his arms around her, and before she could utter an objection, he planted one right on her.

"Ugh! Dave!" she said, pulling away and looking horrified while trying to fix her hair. She pulled out a monogrammed hankie to dab at her lipstick. "What are you doing?" She looked around to see who was watching, and I couldn't stop laughing. It was all perfect.

At the end of the night, as people finally started to leave, Michael came up to me one last time. We wouldn't see each other that night, or until we met at the altar. Tradition in the

North and South alike. He took my hand. "I love you," he said. "And I can't wait to see you tomorrow."

"I'll be the one in the white dress," I said, and winked. We went to our separate rooms.

And to my mother's credit, she didn't actually tell a soul—except Meredith. And I probably would have told her, anyway.

#cawfeetawk

Timing is everything, even when it's off. Take life as it comes and always thank God for unanswered prayers.

Chapter 20

I'M MARRYING BOTH OF YOU

I didn't have cold feet; I guess I owed that to my unborn baby. Cold feet were no longer an option. I loved Michael and was committed to making this work, but I was already living for this baby. The only thing I worried about was Michael. Would he be okay? Was he willing to make this work right alongside me? And would the wedding go off without a hitch? Would some disaster befall us? An earthquake? A flood? Would someone stand up and scream, *I object*? I worried about all these things, but cold feet? No way. I couldn't wait to be married. I was ready to do this because our family was already started.

The morning of the wedding, my mother, my sisters, and I had our hair done at a local salon. Finally, that "bridal" moment I had been waiting for. The muss and fuss over me. Everyone sipped mimosas at a chic salon while people fawned over me.

"What does your dress look like?"

"Where are you going on your honeymoon?"

"Is your husband-to-be handsome?"

The morning was perfect—until I heard it. A sound so familiar and so indistinguishable from any other sound, a sound that can stop even the most eager bride in her tracks. A sound made for ruining happy moments. A sound that has echoed through special family ceremonies for centuries. The sound of a disappointed Jewish mother.

"I hate it! I absolutely hate it," my mother shrieked from across the room. I spun around in my chair. Carolyn was attempting to talk my mother off a ledge. "It's awful. I can't walk down the aisle like this. I look like Gidget!" She was staring into a big mirror in horror because of . . . yes, her hair.

When my mother dislikes something, she obsesses about it. You would think that on my wedding day, she would suck it up and let it go. Not a chance. She hated her hair and everyone within Jersey earshot was going to know about it. The mortified hairdresser looked around for anyone who could *make it stop*. (Southern people aren't used to people making a scene. It is an extreme social faux pas.) But my mother had no intention of stopping. She didn't give two shits about social graces. She just wanted to like her hair (which, incidentally, looked totally fine).

"Ma, it's fine. Leave it alone," I pleaded, but to no avail. She was too far gone. She couldn't stop talking about it. Instead of just saying, *It's fine. I don't really like it but I don't want to upset Jaime*, she decided this was worse than the stock market crash that caused the Great Depression. It would be all I fucking heard *all day*. No matter what I said, she would say something like, "Well, at least *your* hair turned out nice!"

Finally, my sister Carolyn, who was a hairdresser, intervened. "That's it," she said. "I can't take this for one more second. You're ruining her whole day. Get in here and I'm going to redo it." She wet my mom's hair in the sink and blew the whole thing out again.

My mother emerged from the bathroom in a fog of Aqua Net. "Now, doesn't that look bettah?" she said. "My dawtah knows how a mothah of the bride needs her hair to look!" At that point, I didn't care if she came out bald. I just needed her to shut up, so I confirmed her opinion.

"Ma, it looks fantastic," I said, even though it looked exactly like it did before—kind of like a scooter helmet.

She clapped her hands together. "*Now* we can get married!"

We met my brother, David, at the entrance to the sanctuary. He was in a tuxedo and looked so handsome, standing there where my father should have been. I smiled through tears and took his arm, and he walked me down the aisle. I felt like everything was moving in slow motion. Everyone I knew, and a lot of people I didn't know, stood up and watched me. Almost everyone was smiling, and some were crying. I even saw Carole dab at her eyes with her trusted and properly monogrammed handkerchief.

As we stood there in the church, in front of the priest, he asked us to kneel down at the altar. We were each holding candles in the dimly lit church, the setting sun casting an orange glow through the stained-glass windows. The priest's voice droned through the ceremonial rhetoric, and Michael turned, leaned in close, and whispered to me: "I'm marrying both of you."

My heart skipped a beat. For someone who proclaimed himself "not a man of sentiment," with those five words he did something for my heart that no one else had ever done. I was more in love at that moment than I ever knew possible. It was the first time he had acknowledged that a baby was coming, that I was pregnant, and that we were a family. The three of us. He was fully in it, right there with me. This was my new family. This was now the most important thing in my life.

We stood, said our vows, and the priest pronounced us husband and wife. We kissed, and I threw my arms around Michael and never wanted that kiss to end. We walked out of the church hand in hand as my Jersey contingent clapped and hooted and the southerners smiled politely and a little uncomfortably. As an ode of respect to my father, the organist began "Hava Nagila," and I could see my uncle smiling. Michael and I ducked out the door and greeted everyone as they exited the church. The limo took us to the country club (Carole's choice) for our evening reception (my choice).

The wedding reception was an odd mix of northern and southern traditions. I got my black tie and I got my DJ, but when I walked into the reception and saw a table piled with gifts, I wondered whose birthday it was. In Jersey, you don't bring presents to the wedding. You bring an envelope with cash or a check, but never a present. In the South, apparently you cart those white lacy wrapped gifts all the way to the wedding and pile them on a big table.

When all my Jersey family and friends walked in, they looked equally confused. "Where do we sit?" my sister said. "Where are the place cards?"

"I guess you sit wherever you want to sit," I said.

"But . . ."

"I know," I said. "Just roll with it."

Then the DJ made an announcement over the speaker system: "Everybody put your hands together for Mr. and Mrs. Michael Sullivan!" Everyone clapped and the music began blaring through the speakers. I looked at Michael, and he actually grinned and raised his eyebrows.

"What?" I said.

"Listen to the song," he said.

I couldn't place the song the DJ was playing. Was it something from our past? Something that marked a romantic moment? It was familiar, but . . . "What is it?" I said.

"It's the Auburn fight song!" he said triumphantly. I thought the vows had made it official, but for him, we weren't married until he heard the Auburn fight song.

"You people are very weird, do you realize that?" I said. I consoled myself, remembering that the DJ had been given explicit instructions to play Bon Jovi.

Marrying into the SEC

What is it about college football in the South? Northerners love football, too, but down south football reaches a whole new level of obsession. Nobody can have a party, or get married, or have a baby, or move anywhere, when there is a big college football game on. I know a girl who was in labor and her husband refused to come to the hospital until it was time to push because he was watching the Iron Bowl. Imagine you were in New Jersey or anywhere up north and something happened—say, a car accident on the highway. If you were interviewing people on the scene and said, "Can you tell us what happened?" I don't care how well the Yankees are doing that year, nobody in the middle of a car accident scene is going to scream, "Go Yankees!" It just wouldn't be appropriate. But in Alabama? No matter how serious the event, somebody is bound to yell, "Roll Tide!"

"Well, the car came down that embankment and killed that man. Roll Tide!"

One morning I woke up to the entire state of Alabama sobbing and moaning and keening and I couldn't figure out why until I looked on Facebook and found out that somebody had poisoned the famous oak trees at Toomer's Corner at Auburn University—after Auburn beat Alabama. I like trees. Trees are good. We need them. But number one, why is everyone practically throwing themselves prostrate on the floor in despair because of some dead trees, and number two, why the hell would anybody kill some very nice old trees because of football? It's weird. It's just weird. And then there is Bear Bryant. People name their dogs Bear. I know one couple who named their kids Bear and Bryant. That's real.

So when they played the Auburn fight song, I guess I wasn't really all that surprised. It was tradition and there wasn't much I could do about it. At least nobody got hurt.

When the real music started, I immediately wanted to dance. I spun away from Michael onto the dance floor, but nobody joined me. Too soon? I gradually slowed it down, a little embarrassed, and casually walked off the dance floor to the beat. Instead, I decided to focus on Michael.

If the dancing didn't start in the first hour, at least I was vindicated many times over for the arguments I had had with Carole. Michael loved the whiskey bar I ordered. I hadn't told him about it. It was set up out on the patio with high-end Scotch, bourbon, rye, and hand-rolled cigars. He was in awe of it. And the groom's cake was a big golf bag made of chocolate. Everyone told me not to spend the nine hundred dollars, but I did it anyway, and he loved that, too. He kept looking at me like he couldn't believe I knew him so well, and I'd never seen him smile so much in a single four-hour period.

Finally, after a few drinks, my Jersey friends and family got up to dance with me. My mom was shaking it on the dance floor, David was going all-out, and Meredith and Carolyn were out there with me, too. I was having the best time, whooping and hooting and doing my Jersey fist pump. Every time I danced past my grandmother, she would stop me. "These are not our people, Jaim-alah! I don't know how you're going to do this!"

"It's okay, Gram. Just keep dancing!"

At one point, I stepped back from the dance floor and watched them—my beautiful, loud, raucous crew. My ride-or-die team. Sure, it is true that they have no filter, and it is true that they don't always realize when and where it is appropriate to say something or say nothing. But they are mine, and I am theirs. I watched Carole watching them, and just for a second I was a little embarrassed by their behavior. But I shook it off. My grandmother was right. The Sullivans had not been my people yesterday, but now they were stuck with me, and I was stuck with them. Michael, on the other hand, was definitely my people. And we were all going to have to work out our differences if we wanted to survive and learn to love one another.

After the reception, we said good-bye to each person who loved at least one of us, and we made our way to the bridal suite. We walked through the lobby, Michael in his tux and I in my dress. We got onto the elevator to take us up to our wedding suite. It was just the two of us at last. I leaned into his chest.

"Hi, husband," I said, grinning.

"Hi, wife."

We walked down the long hallway and I remembered that time in New York when Michael had been so reluctant to let me inside his hotel room. Not tonight. Michael opened the door to our suite and guided me inside.

I turned to face him. "Here's something I hope I'll never have to say again," I said.

"What's that?" Michael said, moving closer.

"Can you help me out of this wedding dress?"

It was awesomely romantic. We kissed, and then, suddenly, we both stopped, having the same thought at the same time: *Are we allowed to have sex with a baby in there?*

"Is it okay to do this?" Michael asked.

"I don't know!" I said. "I've never been in this situation before."

"But we have to. It's our wedding night," he said.

"We don't *have to*," I said. "A lot of people don't. They're too tired or too drunk."

"But that's not us," he said. "Don't you want to?"

"I *really really* want to," I said.

"But I don't want to hurt the baby," he said. "What if I poke him in the face?"

"I think he's just a grain of rice right now. I'm not sure he even has a face."

"But still . . ." he said.

"I'm calling Meredith," I said. I grabbed the hotel phone and called Meredith's cell. We'd already discussed my secret.

"Hello?"

"Meredith! It's Jaime," I said breathlessly. "Is it okay for us to have sex? We don't want to hurt the baby!"

"Oh my God," Meredith said. "Hang up the phone right now and go have sex. It's fine!"

And so we did.

I could sit and ponder what our wedding, our reception, our wedding night, or our honeymoon in Italy might have been like if I hadn't been pregnant, but that wasn't our experience, so that would be a waste of time and I wouldn't change it for a thing. The pregnancy imbued our early marriage with a sacredness that I loved. Michael was nervous but wanted more than anything to protect me. Here was this man, so confident and successful, at forty-four years old, suddenly married to a woman who was having his baby, and he took none of it for granted. We belonged to him now, and he would fiercely guard us and keep us safe.

I also suspect that our marriage might not have been as successful had God not bound us together in the ways that He did. We had both come to marriage with hesitations and baggage, and while we both wanted to be together, I'm not entirely sure we would have been able to do it. There are people who long for monogamy and eternity, but Michael and I were never those people. So while I might not have chosen it exactly the way it happened, I think that it had to happen that way. I thank God for unanswered prayers and I thank Him for giving me the things I never knew I wanted.

In those early newlywed months, when Michael and I had our troubles, I would sometimes think, *Well, I could be a single mom, just me and my one kid. We could make it.* That was my solace. Then BAM, I got pregnant again. God said, *Guess what? You're not going to do it alone. And if you think two is easy, then BAM, I'm going to give you three.* Over the next few years, God threw children at us like darts, and that bound us together like nothing else ever could have.

But I'm getting ahead of my story.

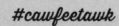

#cawfeetawk

Our "people" aren't always family. Sometimes they're the ones we choose, and the ones that stay, even when things don't go as planned.

Part Three

SOUTHERN METAMORPHOSIS

The value of marriage is not that adults produce children,
but that children produce adults.

—PETER DE VRIES, AMERICAN AUTHOR

A baby is God's opinion that the world should go on.

—CARL SANDBURG, POET

Chapter 21

IT'S A BOY! OR IS IT?

We sat down around the table in my mother-in-law's favorite restaurant—it was dimly lit and classy with white tablecloths and sparkling crystal—and I nudged Michael. We were back from our honeymoon and it had been a few more weeks. It was time to tell them.

"Mother, Pop . . . Jaime and I are having a baby."

"That's wonderful, Mike! So wonderful!" my father-in-law said.

I looked expectantly at Carole but she wouldn't look at me. She was looking at her hand. *She was counting on her fingers.* She looked at Michael. "How far along is she?" she said. *As if I wasn't sitting right there.*

"Well, she's almost twelve weeks," Michael said.

"I see," she said.

Shit. We should have fudged the dates.

"Twelve weeks," she repeated. *Really?* My mother falls on her knees in the grass and sobs, and all my mother-in-law can do is the math. Michael knew exactly what she was thinking. "Mother, we found out she was pregnant six *days* before. This was no shotgun wedding."

"It could have had . . . some effect on your decision," she said. She was grasping at straws. Even a wedding had not fully initiated me into this family. She was still trying to get Michael out of this.

"Noooo," he said, with an emphasis and force that made me love him even more. "We were going through with it, no matter what. This was just a . . ." He looked at me. "A bonus," he said.

She was quiet for a long moment. Plotting. "Well," she said at last. "I think it's better if we just kept this to ourselves."

"Okay, great," I said. "When I start to show, I'll just tell everyone I'm eating myself to death."

Michael and I went for an ultrasound the following week. I was so excited to finally see who was in there. "It's a boy," the ultrasound technician said. Of course it was. Michael was one of five boys, and every single one of them who'd already had children had had boys. There were eleven boys in the family, and not one girl child. Michael grinned from ear to ear and all I could think was, *Carole will be so disappointed.*

My mother-in-law had always wanted a girl. She would never express the depth of this emotion, but being pregnant gave me a new extrasensory perception about these things, and I could see it. I asked Michael if we could wait to break the news to her that it was another boy, but he assured me she would not be disappointed. I was not convinced. When we had lunch with her a few days later, Michael shared the news.

"Wonderful. A son. That is wonderful, really. It is," she said as she hugged Michael. To her credit, she seemed sincere, but I couldn't help but wish we were sharing different news. As much as she and I struggled, I wanted it for her. It was my first baby, and it didn't matter to me one bit what we had, so long as the baby was healthy. But wouldn't a girl bring the two of us closer together? We could be three women, bonded together in a sea of Sullivan men. I decided that I would work on that for the next baby.

A few weeks after the ultrasound, Michael had a golf weekend, and I went to New Jersey. Those were our hobbies, golf and Jersey, and they made us happy. My sisters and brother were there. Meredith was working in the ultrasound department at the hospital and invited me to come to work with her. "I want to see my nephew," she said. "I'll take some cool ultrasound pictures for you."

By this time, I was twenty weeks' pregnant, so Meredith said she could do what she called the anatomy scan. I lay down on the table and she squeezed the jelly on my belly and we both looked at the monitor. "There's the head," she said.

"Does he have a brain?" I asked.

"Of course he does. Right here. It looks so good!" she said. She measured his head. She looked at his face. "He's so cute!" she said. "See, here's his nose. And here's his little four-chambered heart." We both watched it for a minute, enraptured by the sound of the beating. "Ten fingers," she said. "Ten toes. And . . . well, that's interesting . . ."

"What? *What?*" I said.

She looked more closely. "Hmm," she said.

"Oh my God, what?! Is it something terrible?"

"Look at this," she said.

I looked. "What is it? It kind of looks like a hamburger."

"It's definitely not a hot dog," she said.

"*What does that mean?*" I said.

"It means he's a she."

"What?"

"It's a girl," she said.

"No. Way," I said. "Are you sure?"

"I am one hundred percent sure that you are having a girl," she said.

"One hundred percent?"

"One hundred percent."

"How does that happen? Did he switch? Did he change into a girl? Oh my God, what if he didn't change all the way? Could that happen?"

"She didn't switch," she said. "She's always been a girl. Somebody just read the ultrasound wrong. This is definitely not a boy. That," she said, "is a vagina."

She put the image in 4D, which was incredibly detailed and realistic looking, and printed it out. "What do we do now?" I asked.

"I guess you should tell Michael," she said.

So I called Michael. He was on the golf course, and we put him on speaker.

"Hey, bro!" said Meredith.

"Hi, Meredith," he said.

"I have some news for you."

"What's that?" he said. I could hear his golf buddies talking in the background.

"It's a girl," she said.

"What is?" he said.

"Your baby."

There was a long silence. Finally he said, "No, it's not."

"Yes, it is," she said. "It's definitely a girl."

"I have to go," he said.

"What was that about?" Meredith said.

I sighed. "That's just Michael. In fact, that's how his whole family reacts to news until they can figure out what they think about it. They are masters of the disappointing reaction. But I guess this one was probably a pretty big shocker."

I knew Michael wanted a boy. I felt bad for him, but not *that* bad. I decided it was my job to make him feel good about it, so I had a little pink luggage tag made with the name Olivia Susan Carole Sullivan on it—the name we had decided on before the first ultrasound, on the very off chance it would be a girl. The luggage tag thing is very southern, all part of the great tradition of monogramming things. I had also decided that my daughter would have Carole's name as a middle name because, well, if I'm being honest, I knew it would win me points. And just to be fair and balanced, I included my mom's name as well. It actually worked perfectly because with four names, it made it much harder for people to monogram things, which was just fine with me. It was one tiny rebellion. But the luggage tags I could handle.

The next day, I flew home from New Jersey and met Michael and his parents at a restaurant. I knew Michael wouldn't have said anything to his mother yet. It wasn't his way, and I was practically giddy with the knowledge that I had something my mother-in-law wanted more than anything else in the world. And she didn't even know it yet.

At dinner, when I couldn't wait another moment, I turned to Carole. "I have something for you that I brought from New Jersey."

"What is it?" she said, looking at me suspiciously.

I gave her an envelope, and she opened it and pulled out the luggage tag.

"What is this?" she said.

"It's a girl," I said. I tried to hold back a smile.

She looked me in the eye, probably for the first time ever. Her eyes widened. She was in shock. "Pardon me?" she said.

"It's a girl," I said.

"It's . . . a *girl?*" she said, disbelieving.

"It's a girl."

"A girl."

"Yeah, a girl."

I'm not kidding, this went on for a solid five minutes, which is a long time to keep saying the same thing. She couldn't allow herself to believe me. Was I playing a cruel trick on her? No, I was not. With every *It's a girl*, I heard her voice change and run through a whole spectrum of emotion, a whole lifetime of emotion. And then it was like the Tin Man from *The Wizard of Oz*. One tear dropped from her eye. I briefly wondered if she would rust and we could keep her that way.

Then she said it again, but no longer as a question.

"It's really a girl."

"Yes," I said.

Then she looked at Papa Dave, back at me, and finally to Michael.

"Oh, Mike. It's a girl! I can't believe it!"

"Yes," he said, and I could see that it was all okay with him, too. It was all worth it to see his mother so happy. "Isn't that nice?"

"I'm having a girl!" she marveled.

"I'm not here," I said, throwing up my hands. "Apparently I have actually disappeared."

But I would take the high road. I was a new woman, a mother-to-be, and that made all the difference. For my next ultrasound with Dr. Huggins, I thought it would be nice to invite my mother-in-law. Ultrasounds didn't exist back when she was pregnant, so I thought she might like to have that experience. And it also might not hurt for her to physically see that "her baby" was actually located inside my uterus—not Michael's uterus, not her uterus, and not anybody else's uterus but mine.

I took her to the office and she seemed unsure and a little uncomfortable with just the two of us together, but once I brought her into the room, all her attention was on the screen. As I got into the obligatory robe, I whispered to the ultrasound technician, "Look, if you see a penis and my sister was wrong, *don't say a word!* Once the baby is actually here, if there was a mistake, what's she going to do, say she doesn't like him? But she has to believe for now it's a girl. Use some kind of secret sign or something." She laughed. I think she didn't realize how dead serious I was.

But once she fired up the machine and we were under way, she confirmed what Meredith had told me. "Just so you know, it really is a girl," she said. She addressed my mother-in-law when she said this, not me, God bless her.

After that, my mother-in-law softened toward me a little bit. She began to look at me more often, and even address me directly now and then. She sometimes introduced me as Michael's wife—although not yet as her daughter-in-law.

But hey, it was progress.

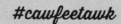

#cawfeetawk

Sometimes curveballs throw us right onto the path we are meant to be on. . . .

Just go with it.

Chapter 22

SCARLETT—MY
EMERGENCY CONTACT

*B*eing married to a Sullivan and also pregnant gave me a new feeling of belonging. I walked around Alabama in a different way. I was still an outsider, still a foreigner. I still talked funny and dressed funny, but I had street cred now. Alabama street cred. I was Jaime Primak *Sullivan*, and as much as it made me cringe to think that a man had given me status I didn't have before, it was true. And it wasn't that he was a man, so much, I told myself. It was that he was a native. He was from Alabama, and so now, as his wife, I could claim ownership over this place in a way I hadn't before.

But the biggest thing I missed was having real, true, bosom-buddy girlfriends. I had them in Jersey, but it's not the same to call someone on the phone as it is to curl up on the couch and eat popcorn and drink wine and sift through the details of life and work and love with a group of girls you can trust. I needed that. I craved it, especially now that I was married and having a baby and feeling like I didn't have the slightest clue what I was doing.

One day, I decided to go to Babies "R" Us, but I couldn't help feeling sad that I was doing it alone. I was registering for my baby shower, and looking at all the baby things. I wasn't actually going to buy anything. It's a Jewish superstition that it is bad luck to buy anything for the baby until it has been born, and like I said: Once a Jew, always a Jew. But I could browse. There was no bad luck in browsing.

I got the baby shower list and wandered around in a daze. Babies "R" Us is an intimidating place when you don't know what you are doing. It's all bright colors and screaming children and plastic toys and baby clothes and gadgets that I would stare at with no idea what they did. I was feeling overwhelmed. I looked at the list and I couldn't even figure out how to fill it out. A woman walked by with two children in her cart, as if she had plucked them off the shelf to buy them. She looked calm and nice and something in me reached out to her. Before I could even think about what I was doing, I found myself saying, "Excuse me. Are you a mother?"

She looked at me, smiled, looked at the children in her cart, and said, "Why, yes I am," as if she wasn't quite sure whether or not I was joking.

"I think I need help," I said. I held out the list to her, plaintively, as if asking a stranger for directions in a foreign country. Those weren't easy words for me to say—they aren't easy in any context—but she never blinked an eye. She didn't ask questions or hesitate or want to know more about me first. All she said was, "Okay. Let me help."

Scarlett showed me how the list worked, and walked me through the entire store and told me what, in her experience, I was likely to actually want, and what wasn't necessary at all. It was such a relief! I don't know what she had planned for her afternoon, whether she was busy and had somewhere to be, any of that. Her children were interested, sometimes offering their own opinions about what was cool or what my new baby might want. They asked if I was having a boy or a girl. They made southern accents sound adorable. And Scarlett was warm and friendly and acted like we'd been friends for years.

That's how Scarlett came into my life. Of all my friends, she makes me feel the safest. She makes me feel like I can go on, no matter what, as long as she is by my side. Sometimes God sends someone into your life exactly when you need them, and they may be with you for just a short while, or they may be with you for the rest of your life. I thank God every day for sending me Scarlett, and I hope she stays in my life for as long as I live. She is a southerner who immediately made me feel at home, rather than making me feel like I didn't belong. She saw me for everything I was, and never for anything I wasn't. She never made me think I should be anything other than myself. She welcomed me into her heart and into her family, and we became friends quickly. Almost immediately, I introduced her to Leigh Anne, and before I knew it I realized that I had a group of friends. It was a small group but by God, it was an actual group! We would do things together. We would hang out and talk about our lives. *We would have girls' night out!* I began to relax into my life a little more because I finally had girls I could talk to, rather than obsessively trying to work out my problems or rationalize my fears in my own head. It really saved me.

Years later, Olivia would tell me, "I love Miss Scarlett. She's like a real mom."

"What do you mean?" I asked her. I wasn't offended. I was curious. What, to my intelligent and inquisitive daughter, did she think of as a *real mom*?

"She's just a *real* mom," she said. "She's safe." I thought about my friends. Most were single or divorced or didn't have children, but Scarlett was the one who was married and drove a minivan just like me. More important, she embraced the role of mother so naturally that she made it look easy, and Olivia recognized that. Scarlett has a calm way about her, a way that allows you to believe everything is going to be okay. She is my emergency contact. She is the one I call when I feel insecure or unsure or nervous or scared. It's Scarlett every time.

#cawfeetawk

You get in life what you have the courage to ask for. I asked for help and I got Scarlett.

– Chapter 23 –

BABY BELLE

*W*hen I was pregnant with Olivia, Carole decided to throw me a baby shower. Or I should say that Carole decided to throw herself a baby shower, and knew she would have to invite me and my kind because etiquette required it. My mother and Meredith flew in, and there were a lot of Carole's friends in attendance, too. People I didn't know but who knew that Carole was finally "having a girl." Leigh Anne and Scarlett were also there.

The shower was a real event for Carole. She put up a big sign across the mantel that proclaimed IT'S A GIRL! in big pink block letters. Now, Carole has thrown many baby showers, but this was the first time she had ever been able to put up that sign, and she was so happy, I couldn't help but feel proud. As the guests arrived, she stood in front of it having her picture taken with everyone, like she was on the red carpet. There are more baby shower pictures of people with Carole in front of that sign than there are of me. I didn't mind. I was proud to give that to her. I knew it would take a grand gesture of this magnitude to move the needle with us, and I was not going to miss the opportunity.

The shower was a catered southern tea, very fancy, with finger sandwiches and petits fours and other tiny foods. After everyone arrived, we all sat nicely, our knees together, sipping our tea and talking politely about the baby. There were no baby shower games. No guessing the mom-to-be's girth, no name-the-baby-game hilarity. No wrapping me up like a pregnant toilet-paper mummy. There was no getting drunk in front of the mom and making jokes about how she can't have any champagne—none of those supposedly crass things we Jersey girls play when celebrating an imminent new person.

Instead, these women talked in hushed voices, as if actually trying not to wake an actual baby, and twittered happily with Carole about grandmotherly concerns and baby girl fashion from beneath their fancy hats. Scarlett and Leigh Anne fit right in, and it amazed me, because they could be such shit-kicking partiers when they wanted to be. Southern cross-training? I watched them talk with Carole's friends. I was impressed.

Meanwhile, my mother and Meredith and I all knew we were out of our element, so we mostly kept our mouths shut. I opened my gifts and everyone oohed and aahed appropriately. In the middle of the present madness, the doorbell rang. One of the guests got up to answer it. "Jaime, it's a present for you!"

Someone handed me the wrapped box with a card attached. I slid the card out of the envelope and read it out loud:

I didn't bring this gift to you myself because I know your baby shower is for women only, but I wanted to send something for the mother of my child. As I looked at your registry, I thought, what could I possibly give her that could even begin to equal what she is giving me? There was nothing, so I picked out this baby monitor, so that even when you and the baby are away from me, I won't have to miss a thing.

"Awwwww!" Everyone melted. The sentiment was too much for an emotional room full of women to bear, and we all got teary-eyed. I unwrapped the baby monitor.

"He's the best husband in the world!" someone proclaimed. Everyone nodded in agreement.

"He's *perfect*," said someone else. They were practically swooning. That's when Carole and I both looked at each other, as if to say, *Oh brother, if only they knew.* It was the first time I think we'd ever really bonded in a meaningful way. We were both moved by Michael's romantic gesture, but nobody knows Michael better than his mother and his wife, and we both knew that no matter how much we loved him, the man was definitely not perfect. To this day, when anyone makes a grand statement about Michael's perfection, Carole and I immediately find each other's eyes.

"He's perfect!" another of the ladies gasped.

Two months later, Olivia was born, and it rocked my world. Everything changed— my priorities, my sense of reality, the size of my boobs, and especially, the size of my heart. I thought I loved my unborn baby, but the real thing was so much more than I ever could have imagined. As I lay in the hospital bed, exhausted from labor and with that tiny new little girl in my arms, everything was perfect . . . well, until *the grandmothers* showed up.

Carole arrived first, and I knew why she was there. I knew

exactly why. Olivia was tightly swaddled in a blanket, and I could see it was killing her not to be able to confirm, without a doubt, that Olivia really was a girl. There was still a tiny needling doubt in her mind. Normally the passive-aggressiveness in which southerners are so well versed eludes me. It feels to me like writing with my left hand. But in this case, I sensed that the direct approach might not be as appealing, so I said, "Carole, would you like to change her diaper?"

"No!" she said, startled by the very suggestion. "No no no no. But . . . you can . . . right now . . . if she needs it . . ."

She wanted to see it so bad.

"Maybe later," I said. I thought she might explode. "Carole. She's a girl," I said. "Really. You can trust me. She's a girl. All right, never mind, I'll change it."

Carole drew nearer, hovering, trying to look uninterested. And then she saw, and she smiled. *At me!* I had actually done something right.

But when my mother arrived, having the two of them in the same room was like worlds colliding. My mother came barreling in like a hurricane. "Where is she? Where is that baby? I need to see that baby right now! Give her to me! Let me kiss her! Let me smother her, I love her so much!" I could see Carole stiffen. It was all too much for her.

"Hi, Ma," I said. "Here she is." I held up the swaddled bundle for her inspection.

"Oh my GAWD, look at her! She's the spitting image of you, Jaime! She's my little Jaime all over again!" She swooped Olivia out of my arms and covered her in Jersey kisses. The kind that resemble a volley of machine-gun fire.

"Okay, Ma, give her back, she's hungry," I said. I made the mistake of deciding to nurse in front of them both.

"Really, Jaime," my mother-in-law muttered, purposefully casting her eyes in the opposite direction. "It's just so . . . can't you just give her a bottle when other people are around?"

My mother agreed. "I'll be honest, we didn't do it in my day, but I think it's very progressive of you, Jaime."

"It's not like this is a new invention, Ma," I said. "People have been doing this since the beginning of people."

"Well, anyway," my mother said, as if I had said something ridiculous, "they say it's a beautiful thing. I think you could be a little more supportive, Carole. If my daughter wants to be modern like that, then that's what she's going to do!"

"Mom, can you keep it down?" I said. "You're always yelling."

"What with the criticism? I'm defending you! Oh, look how big your boobies are! Jaime, you almost look like your moth-ah!" She grinned.

Carole sighed. "I'm just saying it should be a private thing."

"Jaime, I'm so proud of you. When I was pregnant, I smoked, I drank, I played poker, I burped the baby, I had another ciga-rette . . ."

"You did *what*?" Carole said, a look of horror on her face.

"Explains a lot, right?" I joked. Carole obviously wasn't amused.

"Is she latching? What's happening down there?" my mother said, trying to peek under the blanket. "Carole, come see this!"

"Please," Carole said, uncomfortable enough with words like *latching*. She couldn't even look at us.

"Oh my God, people. Stop!" At this point, all I wanted to do was rest. I'd just pushed out a nine-pound baby, I was trying to figure out how to nurse, my boobs hurt, my nipples were sore, I was weak, and the only thing they could agree on was that nobody nursed in their generation.

"I'm happy to leave you alone while you do . . . that," Carole said. She picked up her purse and primly left the room.

"You know, it really wouldn't kill you to give her a bottle, Jaime, if this is so exhausting for you," my mother said.

"Ma. Go." It was all I had the energy to say.

Olivia thrived. Despite my amateur mothering, despite the interference of the grandmothers, despite everything, she got stronger and bigger and more beautiful. She was curious and intelligent and she was always watching us, soaking it all in. I could see her learning, long before she could talk. She amazed me. Sometimes I would gaze at her and I could see myself in her face, and I would dream about our future together, mother and daughter.

Michael, of course, was completely enamored. He was in love all over again, and it was all about her. We were a perfect little family of three . . . for about ten minutes. Because Max.

#cawfeetawk

I've learned that even when people have the best intentions, there will always be opinions that contradict what you feel is right. Do what you feel is right anyway. If they love you, they'll catch on.

Chapter 24

BABY LOVE AND LOSS

When I say God threw babies at us like darts, I wasn't kidding. Eight weeks after having Olivia, Michael and I got pregnant again. He was literally still inside me when he said, "You can't get pregnant yet, can you?"

"Umm, our baby is eight weeks old, so obviously not."

"I didn't think so," he said.

But we were both wrong. When I found out I was pregnant again, and that I was not just pregnant, but pregnant with twins, I burst into tears. It was a mixture of shock and awe. I hadn't even figured out how to be a mommy to my two-month-old and here I was, cooking two more? And I was also terrified. Call me superstitious, but I thought that if I wasn't unambiguously ecstatic about my pregnancy, God might take it away. I didn't tell Michael how I felt. I could see his unbridled joy, and I didn't want to dampen it. Twins! It was his family's crowning achievement. He has twin brothers and nobody else in his family has had twins, so he wanted to be the one. Only twins could trump having the only girl. He was so proud of himself. When he found out, he cried, "I did it!" He looked around for somebody to high-five or fist-bump or whatever it is men do when they feel extra manly.

We already had a short trip planned to the Dominican Republic. Because I'd been pregnant on our honeymoon to Italy, Michael wanted to take me on a trip post-baby so I could really enjoy it. It was a short trip because I was still breast-feeding and pumping, but I was ready and then, well . . . fast-fucking-forward and I'm on another pregnant vacation. This time, I didn't question that I might be pregnant. I knew I was pregnant. I could feel it in every bone and muscle and joint. Then I ate some bad shrimp and had terrible, terrible diarrhea—I'm talking the sweaty, shaking, praying-to-God-for-forgiveness level of sickness. I was sure I'd shit the babies right out and they'd be gone forever.

When we got home, I went for an ultrasound, and there was only one heartbeat. We left the doctor's office and we got into the elevator and Michael started to cry. It was the first time I saw him really cry. I didn't know what to say. I was heartbroken and devastated and still pregnant with one, and I didn't even know what to feel other than guilt and deep, deep sadness.

We decided not to find out whether it was a boy or a girl. Michael said he really wanted it to be a surprise. I don't know which he wanted, but maybe he couldn't stand any more disappointment. The pregnancy was complicated—I had multiple placental lakes (pools of blood in the placenta), so the doctors were concerned and watching me carefully. I felt terrible the whole time while trying to be a good mommy to an infant who needed me.

My whole family flew in for the birth, as was their rowdy tradition, and while I was in labor, Meredith stood by my legs while Michael stood by my head. He didn't ever want to look—he found the whole thing terrifying. Meredith watched the baby come out, and suddenly she burst out, "Oh my God, it's a boy!"

Michael's whole face changed. I saw the shadows lift away. Everyone in the hallway started to cheer. She had said it too loud, they had all heard her! Michael wouldn't get to announce it. His face crumpled. He had waited nine long months for that moment and she had stolen his thunder.

"Oh shit. My bad," she said.

But he couldn't stay disappointed for long. He had his boy. Max came out big and strapping with a heartbeat like a jackhammer. I fell instantly and madly in love. But now, with two babies to deal with, life became exponentially more difficult, and Michael was so in love with the babies that sometimes I felt like he had forgotten I existed.

Eventually, I was giving so much to my babies that I also needed something for myself, so I began thinking about returning to work. I put out some feelers in LA and I found out that there were still some PR things I could be doing, if I was willing to travel. I was. I loved being a mother more than life itself, but I knew that if I didn't also balance that with a career, I would never feel entirely fulfilled. I had to be very honest with myself here. For others, it's different—and right for them—but I knew this is just the way I'm built. So I called my old boss, who hooked me up with a job, and I started traveling to LA occasionally. Michael was more than happy to take the reins when I was gone, and although I welcomed the break, I also missed my children like I was missing an internal organ. And sometimes I felt very far away from Michael.

Fast-forward to when Max was nine months old: I flew to Los Angeles for a client's photo shoot, suffering through a brutal period. The morning of the shoot I noticed something unusual. I continued to bleed while in the shower. Something inside told me this was not normal, but I wasn't overly concerned. I called Dr. Huggins, who immediately began firing questions at me: How long had I been bleeding? Was I in any pain? When was my last period? (Ten days, none, last month—I think?) He told me to come home and come in, so I worked through the photo shoot and caught the next flight home.

I walked into his office in great spirits, feeling at peace as I got started with Paula, the ultrasound technician. Little did I know that my safe little world was about to flip upside down. We both watched the screen as she scanned my ovaries, my uterus. All was good, and then we saw it, both of us at the same time. "What is that?" I asked. "It looks like a gummy bear, doesn't it?" Paula's smile faded as she focused in on the image. "I'm going to need you to stay still, Jaime," she said. There was something about her voice: I knew. I heard it—the familiar, soothing sound of my baby's heartbeat. Her eyes met mine. I desperately tried to search her face for hope. I had an eight-week-old baby growing in my fallopian tube, and there was nothing we could do to change that.

She left the room to get Dr. Huggins and I went into mommy mode. I would leave, I thought. They couldn't force me to do anything. My baby was alive and as long as it was going to try, I would try, too. When Dr. Huggins entered the room, I sat up. "I'm leaving," I said. But he put his hand on my shoulder, telling me, "You can't. It's far too dangerous." I begged him to move the baby, to put it safely in my uterus. He just shook his head. I felt like I was going to throw up. I couldn't focus. I needed Michael. I scrambled for my cell phone, my hands shaking as I dialed his number. I explained to him that I was pregnant but the baby was growing in the wrong place. I needed him to come to the hospital immediately so that he could explain to them that we were keeping our baby. Dr. Huggins gently took my phone and stepped into the hallway.

I could hear snippets: "fallopian tubes," "ectopic pregnancy," "about eight weeks along," "rupture." I lay still, staring at the ceiling for what felt like eternity until Michael walked in. His eyes were red and swollen and I knew immediately what was happening. He held me in his arms as I sobbed—for the guilt I felt when I found out I was pregnant with Max, and for this new baby that I so instantaneously wanted, loved, and needed. I sobbed because I knew that my life would forever be "before loss" and "after."

I had surgery to remove the baby and repair my tube. After it was over, I found myself alone in my hospital room, staring out the window into the darkness and wondering how the sun would ever shine again. I felt so empty. It was a sadness that reached every fiber of my being. A nurse came in and offered me food. When I refused, she smiled and said, "Think of the two healthy babies you have at home," before she closed the door behind her. Tears welled in my eyes. My throat burned. I felt outraged, out of control. I wanted to scream at her that the loss of one child is not somehow offset by others at home— that the way a mother's heart works is like having individual hearts for each child, and when one is broken, it cannot be made whole by another. It must heal on its own. But I said nothing. I just cried.

The pain of losing a baby is a pain so heavy and unique, it's hard for others to understand if they themselves have not experienced it—much like the love for a child is its own thing and can never be clearly described, only experienced.

One evening, weeks later, I came over to Michael and I sat down beside him and I took his hand and I laid my head on his shoulder. "I need to have another baby," I said.

"So do I," he said.

After the ectopic pregnancy, Dr. Huggins suggested we wait at least three months before trying to get pregnant again. Michael and I decided to get through the holidays and try again in May so that we might have three January babies. In late April, I went in to see Paula, my ultrasound technician. Because of my ectopic pregnancy, only one tube works, so I wanted Paula to tell me if I was ovulating from the good side. When she gave me the thumbs-up, I went home and Michael and I had sex. Then he left for five days on a business trip. That was on a Thursday.

That next Tuesday, I went to see Paula again, for another ultrasound (because Dr. Huggins obviously indulges all my neurotic whims). I still wasn't ovulating. "I missed my window!" I told her. "Michael is away on a business trip!"

"I thought you would be ovulating by now," she said.

"I'm about to," I said. "I can feel it. I'm ready to pop." (I can always feel when I ovulate. Is that weird?)

I asked Dr. Huggins if Michael's sperm might still be swimming around in there when I ovulated. "No way," he said.

Ten days later, Michael and I were at the beach with the kids and I looked at him.

"I'm pregnant," I said.

"How do you know?"

"Because I know."

When we got home, I bought a pregnancy test, and sure enough, it was positive. "It's a girl," I told Michael.

"How do you know?" he said.

"Because your sperm were still hanging around, and all the boy sperm were dead by then, so it is definitely a girl. A tenacious, stubborn little girl who insists on being born."

"Okay," Michael said. He never knows what to think when I say things like that. I think he's learned to just believe me.

The next day, I called Dr. Huggins. "Guess what?" I said.

"Don't even tell me you're pregnant," he said.

"Oh but I am," I said, hardly able to contain my glee.

"Are you kidding me?" he said. "Well, if you are, then it's a girl."

"I know."

When we broke the news to my mother-in-law, she looked annoyed. "Stop having babies!" she said.

"But Carole, you had five," I pointed out.

"Yes, but that was a different time. You work too much. Why do you want to keep having babies?" I shot her a look. I knew where she was going, and I wasn't having it. By now I had lived in the South long enough to know that getting defensive was not the right tactic here.

"Don't worry, Carole," I said. "It's a girl. Olivia deserves a sister, don't you think?" By now, I knew how to beat her at her own game.

Michael and I were thinking of names; I really wanted to name this baby—boy or girl—after my grandfather who had passed away. His name was Charlie. He was in the navy and he was a boxer—never afraid to fight, in or out of the ring. I thought it was a strong name, and after my issues with Max I thought, *If I'm going to have any complications, I want to give this baby a name that represents strength.*

Beware the self-fulfilling prophecy.

But part of me still feels like I had four children. After the ectopic pregnancy, well-intentioned people would sometimes say, "See? You're getting that third baby." But Charlie was not my third child—she was my fourth. I will always mourn that baby. I will always remember the sound of her soothing heartbeat, and my heart will forever ache knowing she tried so hard to make it work, even when I couldn't.

Chapter 25

ADRIENNE: BECAUSE EVERY BRUNETTE NEEDS A BLONDE

$\mathcal{I}$ met Adrienne when I was pregnant with Charlie, and she was pregnant with Libba, her third child. We were in "mommy and me" gymnastics together with our other children, who were all about the same age, and I was immediately drawn to her. She was quiet and beautiful and blonde—the opposite of me, but definitely my "type." It's no secret that I have always been attracted to women. I don't pursue relationships with them, and I think it's a healthy attraction. Sometimes it is physical, sometimes it feels chemical, other times it is purely emotional, but in the case of Adrienne, it was (uniquely) all three. I pursued her, and although my amorous overtures probably terrified her, all I knew was that I wanted to be her friend.

Maybe one reason I liked her so much at first was that she reminded me so much of Michael. Adrienne is an Aquarius, just like my husband. Their birthdays, as it turns out, are just two days apart, and I already know that Aquarians need very little in the way of emotion. Many of them don't like to be the center of attention—or at least, they don't need to be. They take it all in from the sidelines and think about it. They love hard, but you have to really know one to know that you are being loved because they don't express it in an obvious way, the way I do. Not to get too woo-woo astrology about it, but I'm a Libra, and if I love you, I am sitting on the bar drunk, dedicating Billy Joel songs to you. Aquarians are very different. Their love is internal and that's how they like it.

But let's get back to that first meeting. I noticed two things about Adrienne immediately (besides her similarity to Michael): One, she was way prettier than me pregnant. She was adorable and cute, while I was a fat sweaty mess losing my mind most of the time. Two, she had a very calm way about her, and I felt safe around her, even before I knew her. I am anything but calm, and I wanted more of what she had.

Most of my friends from Alabama are polite and calm, but there was something more about Adrienne. She had an easy energy. As we helped our kids through their toddler gymnastics moves, I quickly noticed how well Adrienne was able to stand back and let her kids try things and fail and then try again, while I was the nervous Nellie helicopter mom, buzzing around Olivia and Max, on top of them the whole time, holding their hands. I was like a bad *Saturday Night Live* skit: "Olivia, do you need help with that somersault? Max, be careful on that trampoline! Here, Olivia, let me hold your hand when you do that! *Oh my God, Max, are you okay?!*"

Then I would notice Adrienne, cool as a cucumber and cute as a button, watching her kids tumble about. She wasn't even flinching. She was just . . . *letting her kids enjoy the experience.* Now that was something I could aspire to. She quickly became my idol.

So after a few classes, I decided I would send her a friend

request . . . in person. Not on Facebook. Eye to eye. I was nervous, like a kid in junior high sending a note: *Will you be my friend? Check yes or no.* "Hi," I said. "I'm Jaime. You seem really cool. Can we be friends?"

She thought it was hilarious. "Sure," she said. And then we were.

But I could tell that while she was as fascinated with me as I was with her, she was also a little scared of me. I was probably putting out this *I'm totally attracted to you* vibe. It's not like I tried to kiss her or hold her hand or anything, but girls can sense these things. Still, she was game to be my friend, and I think I was a curiosity to her—like an exotic zoo animal she'd never seen before, and she wanted to see just what I would do if she threw peanuts at me.

We started hanging out together and getting to know each other, but it was not long after that when I had my eleven-week sonogram. Paula told me something didn't look right with the placenta. "It's right over your cervix," she said.

Dr. Huggins decided that it was still early enough that as the uterus grew, the placenta would grow like a balloon with it.

"I don't think so," said Paula. And she was right.

At thirty weeks, my placenta blew out in the bathroom. Blood was everywhere. It was horrible. Michael rushed me to the hospital, practically naked with a towel between my legs.

I stumbled into the emergency room and a woman sitting by the door screamed, "She's having a baby! She's having a baby in that towel!"

The nurses came running. "Is there a baby in that towel?" one of them screamed.

"Not yet!" I screamed back. "But I have complete previa so it could happen!"

Everything moved very quickly from there. Steroid shots, blood transfusions, catheters. They admitted me and I was instructed to move as little as possible. They told me if I made it through the night, they would have to keep me until Charlie was born. I needed to be on total hospitalized bed rest. I couldn't walk around or do anything but lie there, with Charlie in my belly, passing the days one at a time, praying, talking to her, trying to lie still. But nobody told Charlie to lie still. Unborn, she was already a pistol. She never stopped moving or causing me grief. It was torture and Michael was rarely able to visit me because he was always dealing with Olivia and Max and, of course, his own job. Thank God for my belles. They jumped right in.

Leigh Anne went winter clothes shopping for my girls because she only has boys and never got to shop for girls. She took Olivia to do things that I couldn't do with her and got her ready for her preschool photo. Scarlett came and prayed for me and over me and for Charlie and over my kids, and she also made sure that people who came by brought the snacks that I loved. Leigh Anne came every week without fail to give me a prenatal massage. (Got to love having a masseuse as a bestie!) Scarlett planned a baby shower and filled my hospital room with friends. They kept me sane. They reminded me who I was. And they let me be as Jersey as I had to be to get through this. There were days I yelled, I screamed, I cried, and they sat with me through it all.

But I didn't see Adrienne. Because we were such new friends, she (later) told me she wasn't comfortable coming to visit me yet, when I was in such a severe and frankly traumatic situation, but that she thought of me every day. I didn't blame her—the situation was grim, not just for me but for everyone around me, and I imagined it could be frightening for another pregnant woman. However, while I was on bed rest, she gave birth to her daughter Libba, and one day, she sent me a text message with a picture attached. It said, "Hi, Jaime! I thought you might want to see a picture of Libba. I have to take her for her check-up. Would you mind if we stopped by to visit you?"

I was ecstatic. I opened the attachment, and of course, there was the most gorgeous blue-eyed cherub I'd ever seen. *Of course she would have the perfect baby*, I thought. I was dying to have a visitor, especially one with a baby, so I quickly texted back that I would love to see her, but that I had one condition.

When you are on bed rest for five weeks, there is literally nothing fun to do other than eat, and because I had been trying to shove down as many Rice Krispie treats as was humanly possible, the hospital had cut me off and was trying to manage my diet. This made me crave crazy things, and so I wrote back: *I need a box of baby wipes for my boob sweat and pits, and I desperately need hard Jewish pretzels and a jar of French onion dip.*

That sounds disgusting! she wrote back.

Don't judge me! I whined back. I wasn't sure if she thought my boob sweat was gross or that hard pretzels and French onion dip was not a food combination anyone should enjoy, but either way, I needed to clarify one more important point: *One more thing: I'm not supposed to have food like that, so you're going to have to sneak it in*, I typed.

Now, if you have never lived in the South or known any really genteel southern women, I need to explain exactly what I was asking of her. Asking a southern woman to break rules is a true test of friendship because they don't want to break rules. They are literally raised to follow the rules. They take that shit seriously.

Will we get in trouble? she texted back. *What if we get caught?*

We won't get caught. Just put them in the diaper bag or something.

Finally I persuaded her to do it.

The first thing I noticed when she walked in was that, just a few weeks after giving birth, she was wearing fucking skinny jeans. There are certain people you see in their pre-pregnancy jeans a few weeks after they give birth and all you can think is, *I hope someone kidnaps you and ties you down and forces you to gorge on doughnuts for the rest of your life*. Others you think with all sincerity, *Good on you, girl!* That's how I knew I really was in love with her—I was so happy for her that she was wearing her skinny jeans. "Did you get the stuff?" I whispered conspiratorially.

She nodded, looked nervously around, then carefully lifted up four very expensive-looking blankets she had wrapped all around her perfect baby, swaddled in the car seat, and there they were.

I laughed. "You hid them under the baby? You could have just put them in the diaper bag."

"The diaper bag is the first place they would look! I didn't want to get caught!"

"You're not going to get caught," I said, tearing open the bag and diving in like a Hungry Hungry Hippo.

"How do I know I'm not going to get caught? I've never done a mission before!" she said. A mission? How adorable is that? (I was infatuated. I had imprinted on her like a were-wolf.)

When a nurse peeked in around the door to see if I needed anything, Adrienne threw a monogrammed pink blanket right over the pretzels and open jar of dip, like the cops were raiding us and we were breaking up dime bags. The blanket was all in the dip—ruined for sure. "Fine, fine, everything is fine, no food here, just hanging out with my baby!" she said, her voice a high-pitched shriek.

"Real smooth, Adrienne," I said, as the nurse shut the door. I pulled back the pink blanket and scraped dip off—was it cashmere?—with a chunk of pretzel. "Want one?"

"Ew," she said, crinkling her nose. She was more interested in the mission. "That was a close one!"

"You know they can't do anything to us, right?"

She shrugged. "You never know!" She glanced at the door, her hands hovering over the blanket, ready to cover up the evidence again if necessary. I realized it was probably the most exciting thing that had happened to her all day, and she was taking it all very seriously, her role as accomplice. You know how you go through an experience with a friend and you know that it seals the deal? Because they've seen you at your worst and been all in, anyway? That was when I knew that if the shit ever goes down, Adrienne would go down with me.

After that little adventure, Adrienne stowed everything back up under the baby. "Throw it in the garbage!" I said.

"No evidence left behind!" she crowed.

"If I knew you were going to be this good, I would have had you sneak in an Entenmann's!" I said.

"What's an Entenmann's?" she said.

"Oh my God, never mind," I said. (Apparently, southern people don't eat Entenmann's. I can barely comprehend this.)

Just after Adrienne left, my mother-in-law arrived. We had planned for her to bring me a sampling of smock dresses for Olivia to wear at Thanksgiving. Because this is what is important when you are lying in the hospital. But I knew it was important to her, so I had to let her do it. It made her feel like she was helping me, even though I would never in a million years put a smock dress on Olivia. Apparently that, too, is a southern thing that all little girls are supposed to wear.

When my mother-in-law walked into the room with her armful of little dresses, I told her my new friend had just left.

"Tell me all about her," my mother-in-law said. "Who are her people?"

All I had to say was, "She went to Mountainbrook High School and she lives in Crestline," and my mother-in-law loved her as much as I did. Those are buzzwords for her, like when normal people see something about Brad Pitt or Jennifer Aniston in a tabloid. *Ooh, tell me more!* So we talked and she began showing me the dresses, and then all of a sudden, I started to feel unwell.

"Carole . . . can you come back tomorrow?"

"What? No, I have back-to-back appointments. I thought we were doing the dresses," she said. I could tell she was hurt, but I didn't want to worry her, and I didn't want anyone to know that I was probably having a contraction. Although I'd been on bed rest for five weeks, I just wasn't ready, and if I told anybody, it would become real. Carole packed up the dresses and left me, and I closed my eyes and I contracted on and off all night. I kept moving the monitor off my stomach to throw the nurses off my trail—I'm still not totally sure why. Maybe I was so used to trying *not* to go into labor that it was force of habit, but the doctor had told me I needed to get to thirty-four weeks, that was the goal, and today was *exactly thirty-four weeks. Technically* I had made it, but the warrior in me wanted to keep her in. Couldn't the baby stay put just a little bit longer? I felt like neither of us was ready—not Charlie, and not me. But Charlie apparently didn't agree. The nurses kept coming in to check on me and making friendly comments like, "Boy, this baby sure is active tonight." They had no idea. Yes, I was already using my kid as a smokescreen, letting her take the fall for my bad behavior.

Finally, the next morning, I called Michael. "Listen," I whispered. "I've been having contractions. I'm going to try very hard to stay still, but I don't know how much longer things are going to stay stable." I spent the day on my side watching *Sex and the City* reruns. Around 5:00 PM, my contractions started to intensify. I knew I wouldn't be able to keep the situation a secret much longer. And then, in what was possibly the worst timing ever, Carole breezed back into the room. I looked at her in horror. I'd forgotten I had told her to come back tomorrow. What a mistake. I was going from bad to worse.

"What?" Carole said, seeing the alarm on my face.

And then, all of a sudden, I felt a gush. I knew it couldn't be my water breaking because I had complete placenta previa and the placenta was blocking my cervix. If my water had broken, it wouldn't be able to gush out like this. I knew it was blood. My blood. I had to stay calm, so very steadily, I said, "Carole, I need you to go out into the hallway."

"What do you mean? Why? I need to show you these dresses," she said, and she started to drape them around the room so I could see.

"*Carole*," I said, my voice firmer. I knew this was it. My body couldn't wait any longer. It was now or never, and I already knew I was headed for an emergency C-section and PICC lines and a blood transfusion. And I didn't want her to see all that. "Get me a nurse."

She looked at me, then she looked at the dresses, and then it seemed to dawn on her. She turned around and ran out into the hallway to the nurse's station, and I heard her say, "My daughter-in-law needs somebody!"

A nurse peeked in. "What's going on, Jaime?"

"Is Dr. Huggins on the floor?" I asked, as calmly as I could.

"Yes, I think so."

"Please page him. It's an emergency."

I took deep slow breaths and clenched my fists, and when Dr. Huggins walked into the room, I told him what I knew: "I'm in labor."

"Why do you think you're in labor, Jaime?" he said kindly. He was so used to humoring me. Slowly, I stood up, and there it was—blood, soaking my clothing, the bedding, everything.

Everything began to move very quickly. Nurses were running in and out, jabbing me with giant needles, my mother-in-law was getting tossed around in the hallway as medical personnel rushed back and forth. At the most frantic possible moment, a sweet lady from the Service Guild, who had signed up to bring me food, steps into the room. "I've got your dinner and . . . oh, oh, oh, dear, okay, I'll leave it right outside, oh God!" she said, backing out of the room clutching a casserole dish.

Then I was on a gurney, being wheeled toward the operating room, and I heard my mother-in-law on the phone with my father-in-law. Where was Michael? I fumbled for my phone. "Babe, what are you doing?" I said.

"I'm about to put Max and Olivia in the bathtub," he said.

"You better get here now," I said. "I'm going in."

My in-laws were there when I was rushed in for the emergency C-section, and Michael made it to the hospital just in time to see the birth. At thirty-four weeks and one day, Charlie was born, weighing six pounds even. She was a beautiful blue-eyed baby. I thought, *What are the chances? Three kids, three completely different eye colors.* They were Michael's eyes (and they still are).

When I got out of Recovery and they moved me back to my room, I was depressed and sad because Charlie was in the NICU. I was a complete mess. Michael went down to the NICU to be with her and I took a selfie, and I looked like I had been run over by a truck. I texted it to Adrienne with the caption: *They found out you brought those pretzels in. This is what they did to me.*

OMG did you have the baby??? she texted back.

Yes, I wrote. *It was the pretzels and the dip. The dip did it. It's all your fault.*

And then, Adrienne and I were both mothers of three.

Nobody in Adrienne's world understood our friendship. Her family thought I was too abrasive and her friends didn't see the attraction. Her friends are all very lovely. I wouldn't describe myself as lovely. Nobody got it on her side, but on my side, everybody got it, because she was just like Michael, and my need for calm in all my insanity was obvious to everyone. Michael and I didn't make sense, but then again, we did—and if Michael and I made sense on some level, then Adrienne and I made sense, too.

I remember the first time Adrienne invited me to one of her clubs. She's one of those people who is in a dance club, a book club, a supper club, a garden club. She is also one of those people who, just like most of her friends, knows whether you live on the high side of the street or the low side of the street. She knows all the good stuff southern women are supposed to know. So when she wanted to debut me to her friends, I thought she would be nervous. But no, she wasn't nervous at all. I remember sitting down with all these perfect-looking southern women, all of them staring at me like they were at the zoo and I was some new species of animal put on display. As Adrienne passed out the drinks and did the whole hostess thing, I swear she was wearing a look of pride, as if to say, *Yep, that's my new animal. I'm really proud of her. She's doing quite well here. Everybody line up and take a look and if you're lucky, you will hear her speak!*

I thought she would be embarrassed by me or that she

would worry about what might come out of my mouth, but she wasn't. I'm sure I said a million wrong things and I'm sure I said things that made them all feel uncomfortable. At one point, I asked one of the women, who had just had twins that were still in the NICU, about what position she uses to nurse them both at the same time. Nobody answered, and clearly, all the women were put off by the question, but Adrienne just smiled at me, as if to say, *Good for you, you were really putting yourself out there, trying to make conversation.* Frankly, for me, the zoo animal, it was not exactly the way I'd choose to spend an afternoon. But I did my best. For her sake. Because I loved her.

After it was over, I couldn't help asking her: "Why the hell did you invite me to that whatever-it-was? Because I'll be honest, I definitely felt out of place and everybody else felt it, too."

"You're not going anywhere in my life, and the only way my other friends will ever understand is if they get to know you. I think you did great."

"Really? Because I felt like a moron," I admitted.

"No, no, you were you, and anyone who didn't get you will never get you, and that's fine, but the people who got you loved you. And believe me, some of them loved you," she said. "And that's all you need to know."

The next time Adrienne invited me to one of her girl clubs, I was like, "Hell no, have a good time, call if me if the shit goes down." But I never went back and I never will. That's her thing, and I'm okay with that. I love her for inviting me once and letting me know it could be my thing if I wanted it to be, even though I will never, ever want it to be.

But I did invite her to my thing, and that was travel.

The following October, eleven months after Charlie's birth, it was my thirty-fifth birthday, and I decided I was going to go to Vegas, because . . . where else would I go? All my friends from New Jersey were going, including my sisters, and I decided I would also invite Adrienne. She said she would talk to her husband, Hud, to see if it was okay, since it would mean leaving him with their three kids, and in a few days she called me and said yes, cool, she was going.

This seemed like no big deal to me, but Adrienne's friends were scandalized: *Hud is letting you go to Vegas with that Jersey girl???*

"What do they mean by 'letting you go'?" I asked. "And what do they think Jersey girls do in Vegas, anyway, prostitute themselves? Smuggle small children over the border? Cook meth? What? Am I missing something? Is there some stereotype I don't know of? Do Northern girls kidnap Southern people and take them to Vegas and force them to cheat on their husbands?"

Adrienne just smiled. "What matters is that I'm going," she said.

And she did. We all went to Vegas, and you'll be happy to know that Adrienne survived unscathed. So the travel continued. When my client Chris Klein was promoting his film *American Reunion*, I took Adrienne with me to Los Angeles for the press junket. Naturally, she and I shared a room—a bed, in fact. On the first night, when we were getting ready to turn in, there was a knock on the hotel door. Adrienne rushed to the door, opened it, whispered something quietly, and came back with four pillows.

"What are those for?" I asked.

Without saying anything, Adrienne quietly began to build a pillow wall in the middle of the bed. Suddenly I realized she thought I might try to put the moves on her. I wait for her to build her wall of security made of feathers and cotton. Then I wait for her to lie down. Then I lie down. Finally, I can't help but say something.

"I really don't know what's cuter, that you think I would actually put the moves on you, or that you think a wall of pillows would stop me if I decided to come across this bed."

"Well . . . I had to do something," she said nervously.

We had a great time on the road, and Adrienne quickly became my new travel partner in crime. Once she realized I wasn't going to ravish her, she was eager to go anywhere I needed to go. Whenever I needed an assistant or just someone to hang with, I took her along: New York, New Jersey, Los Angeles, Beverly Hills. She learned more about what I do for work, and we got to be closer than ever.

When I got the opportunity to do *Jersey Belle*, Adrienne was originally supposed to be one of the belles. She was at the top of my list, but when they did the screen tests, the casting director called me.

"Listen, there's an issue with Adrienne," he said.

I was immediately up in arms. "Why? What do you mean?"

"Bravo isn't going to go with Adrienne. She's too quiet, she's got four kids and a new baby, and that's not what this show is about, and we're going to pass on her." No three words had ever affected me the way "pass on her" affected me. I have been in the business for over a decade and have very thick skin, but "pass on her" almost killed me. I had never felt such disdain for the industry that I chose until that moment. This girl had become such an intricate part of my life, such an intricate part of my children's lives, and nobody understood our friendship—not even Hollywood. I thought, *Pass on her? How the fuck do you pass on her? Do you not see what I see? Could you not look a little deeper?*

But I showed them. I managed to sneak her in to almost every episode in some form or fashion, which worked out perfectly because she felt included without having the show derail her entire life like it did for everyone else.

To this day, my undying love for Adrienne is evident every time she walks into the room. Adrienne and I have gone through birth, death, heartbreak, money troubles, insecurities, rebounds, and just about everything else that women can go through together. She teaches me so much. At least three times a week, I call her for advice about social situations, southern traditions, or for Alabama translation, when I don't know what the hell people are talking about. Adrienne is one of the few people who can look at me in public and do a tiny subtle shake of her head nobody else can see, and I know whatever I'm saying or doing is not right. I welcome it—around here, that's invaluable. Like a dog trainer, but she's a Jaime trainer. She gives me these small commands and I follow them and I do the same for her. I like to think I've helped her stand a little taller in her life. When she needs a nudge, when she's stepping out and being assertive or trying something new, sometimes she'll look back at me and I'll give her a little nod: *Go ahead, you're on the right path, you can do it.* People still think we are a little like the odd couple, but to me, Adrienne makes more sense than most things in my life. I knew I didn't want to live in the south without her in my life. I warned her that if she was ever mad at me, I would stand outside her house with a boom box on my head like John Cusack in *Say Anything*. I really do love her.

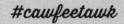

#cawfeetawk

Coco Chanel once said, "Beauty begins the moment you decide to be yourself." I say being yourself may not make you many friends, but it will always make you the right ones.

Chapter 26

CHARLIE

*W*hen she was born, Charlie was a mess. She'd had the cord wrapped around her neck twice, and when she came out, there was a true Boy Scout knot tied in the cord. She went straight to the NICU, and from the very beginning, she wanted so badly to do everything on her own. At even a few days old, she was pulling tubes out of her nose and annoyed by everything. They only let me nurse her for two minutes at a time because they didn't want her to burn more calories than she was taking in. She nursed great, though—and when I tried to unlatch her, she would scream ferociously. She was a fighter from the very beginning, and she's been causing a ruckus ever since.

It's funny how each kid's birth seems indicative of that kid's personality. Olivia came exactly when she was meant to come. It was very formulaic. My water broke, we went to the hospital, I got the epidural, five hours later they told me to push, I pushed a few times, and out she came. She slept, she ate, she pooped, and she spent the first year of her life observing and collecting information. Watching from the sidelines on Mommy's hip. Learning the southern ways. Letting my mother-in-law teach her. Understanding the culture as a tiny child in ways I never would.

Max was a surprise, and full of mischief and trouble, but strong and hearty. And Charlie . . . Charlie the beautiful disaster waiting to happen. Of all my children, Charlie physically resembles Michael most, but her personality is *all Jersey, all the time*. Thank God for small favors.

And as it turns out, Charlie is probably my last baby. She is a precious treasure to me, like all of my children, but in knowing that she is my baby, and that every milestone may be the last one I get to encounter, my relationship with her will always be fraught with emotion, built on passion, and drowned in love.

#cawfeetawk

H.O.P.E—Hold On, Pain Ends

Most of us have had those darkest moments, when we are sure that the light will never come again. However, I can promise you that in time, it will. Don't allow anyone to minimize what you are going through. Allow yourself to grieve. We don't ever forget, and we shouldn't have to forget, but we do have the ability to heal around the pain.

Chapter 27

DANIELLE, MY BELLE

*N*ow that I had three children and it appeared I was staying put, I needed my friends more than ever. And slowly but surely, I was also learning to speak their language. We found common ground, Leigh Anne and Adrienne and Scarlett and I. They were southern, but they had many parts to their lives that I could now understand—children, frustration with husbands, jobs they had to balance, self-esteem to juggle, and that very basic female need to *talk it out*.

But I had room in my heart for more, and thank goodness because I hadn't yet met Danielle.

How can I describe Danielle? If an alien came down from outer space and asked to see the quintessential example of a southern belle, we couldn't choose a more representative sample than Danielle. Poise. Grace. Reservation. Elegance. Refinement. Beauty. (Most of the traits I was lacking.)

When I first met her at a coffee shop, our talk was politely guarded. She was gorgeous and sweet, but I could tell she didn't know quite what to make of me. I'd never met anyone who was so perfectly polite. When I asked her about what her husband did, and she began to tell me, I asked, "So, how does his business do? Does he do well?" Being a businesswoman and an entrepreneur, I'm always curious about how other people's businesses fare out there.

She gave me the strangest look, a hilarious mixture of shock, horror, and good manners. "I'm . . . well, I'm not going to answer that."

"Why not?" I said.

"I just don't think it's appropriate," she said, turning an attractive and flattering shade of pink.

"I didn't ask how he was in bed," I said. "Not that I wouldn't," I added. "I'm just talking about business."

She cleared her throat. "Have you noticed how warm it is today?" She fanned herself with her menu.

But for some reason, Danielle found me interesting, and my occasional shocking comments didn't scare her away (except for that one time when I started talking about cervical mucus, and she got up and left the coffee shop without a single word). After our first encounter, I introduced her to Scarlett, Leigh Ann, and Adrienne, and she seemed relieved and heartened to know that other southern girls had vetted me. I soon learned that Danielle is so giving and warmhearted and full of love that she can't hold anything against anyone for very long. I had much to learn from her. When a mutual friend broke my heart, my initial reaction was to hurt her. (Old habits die hard.) Danielle took me out for a glass of wine and talked me through it. "The most satisfying thing is being the bigger person," she said.

"Really? That's strange, because I'm pretty sure the most satisfying thing would be to donkey-punch her."

Danielle shook her head. "You're a lady, Jaime. You're also a child of God. Act like it."

Shit. How was I supposed to argue with that? I knew she meant it.

She looked around. "See that girl at the end of the bar?" I glanced over. "She's always been very short with me. I could ignore her or act ugly, but I won't. Killing them with kindness is so much more effective."

Killing them? Kindness as a weapon? Now she was speaking my language. That almost sounded *devious*. I wanted to know more! "What do you mean?" I said.

"Oh, just watch." She got up, walked right over to the woman, smiled, made small talk, gave her a quick wave-off, came back, and sat down. She crossed her legs and sipped her wine, and it was hot. I glanced back at the woman at the end of the bar. She looked perplexed, unsure of what had just happened. Maybe Danielle's way wasn't so ridiculous after all. She had scored.

Danielle is quintessentially southern. It's so much more than her outer beauty. It's what she stockpiles on the inside. To her, manners matter. Etiquette matters. Tradition matters. Table settings matter. Beauty matters. She puts sincere appreciation and attention to detail into everything she does. There is no half-assing it in Danielle's world. I'm a beast when it comes to work, but I let a lot of other stuff go. Not Danielle. Everything she does, she does to the best of her ability, including being a friend. She will do anything for a friend. *Anything*. No matter the emotional cost.

Danielle's heartbreaking cross to bear is infertility, and if anyone has love to give a child, it is her. She truly lives her life. She loves. She gives. And she waits. Every day I pray to God to give her what she needs in life, whatever that may be. It's not my call. Maybe it's not even hers. But I can see how it feels to her when she sees her friends with their children, and because she smiles genuinely and goes on while her heart is breaking on the inside, I think she is the strongest person I know. And the more I learn about southerners, the more I understand that Danielle is doing exactly what a southern belle is raised to do: withstand *anything*, no matter how terrible, with grace and dignity. Now, that's something I can really admire.

#cawfeetawk

Some people are meant to teach you. Danielle is one of those people. Nobody could do a better job of teaching me about southern manners, and I can think of no better person to teach my children the ways of the South. There isn't a day that goes by that I don't tell her how much I love her. She is grace personified, and she is my southern belle idol.

Chapter 28

SAVED BY THE BELLES

There have been many times in my journey when I didn't think I would make it, and when I look back, I see that the southern belles I call my own have been the ones who have pulled me through. Michael is always there, of course, and God is always above me, holding out His arms; but when I am down in the trenches, when the survival tactics of "old Jaime" rear their ugly heads, I call on my belles, and they pull me back to the Jaime I want to be. They have talked me off ledges, made me laugh when I wanted to cry, picked up my kids, brought me soup and cookies, shared bottles of wine with me, endured my bad language, allowed themselves to be embarrassed by me, even accompanied me back to Jersey. Collectively, they are my rock.

Especially when I doubted my marriage.

Believe it or not (some won't), sometimes it's hard to be married to Michael Sullivan. He is the perfect father, especially in the eyes of my children. They adore him to such an extent that when he comes home, they don't even see me anymore. He gives everything to them, which sometimes can mean there is nothing left for me. He is handsome, successful, and sometimes, actually often, emotionally distant. It's hard to get a rise out of him, and that frustrates my scrappy side. And sometimes, I just feel alone. There was a time in my marriage when I really wasn't sure whether we were going to make it, when I was taking it week by week. It took a toll on my self-esteem.

I am a lover. I am big and bold and physical. I want hugs and kisses and affection and sex and adoration, and that's not Michael's way. He is not aggressive or forward or physical or even a sex initiator. He says things like, "Babe, just let me know when you want it, and I'm happy to oblige." He couldn't understand, no matter how many different ways I explained it, that women need to feel the chase. We need to feel desired. I make power decisions at work all day; I don't want to be the boss at home. At one point, I began to doubt our marriage could work, and I shut down.

It was Danielle who helped me see that I might be playing a role in our problems. "Maybe you think it will be easier to leave if you push him away," she suggested.

"Oh," I said, realizing she might be right.

"Don't make it so easy on yourself," she said. "I really don't think that's what you want. You might want to leave Alabama, but you don't want to leave Alabama without Michael."

And she was absolutely right.

It was Leigh Anne who took me out to party when I needed a girls' night out. It was Scarlett who took the kids when I decided Michael and I needed to have a date night and reestablish some lost intimacy. It was Adrienne who was the most unexpected foot soldier for me, the one who cried with me at three AM, who stood by me through everything that having three kids and a husband in a strange land requires, and for whom I thank God at least seven times a day.

And surprisingly, it was my mother-in-law, the matriarch of the belles in my life, who finally made sure I would stay.

My mother-in-law has been both my nemesis and my greatest teacher. It took us both a long time to understand each other. What I didn't realize at first was that God was giving me the best possible teacher to guide me through my new life. I couldn't have asked for a better pilot to help me navigate the South, and especially to help me raise my future southern daughters.

But she would also save me, many times over. The first time Michael and I had a fight that was so serious, I thought it warranted my leaving forever, I didn't know where to go, and found myself mysteriously driving to my mother-in-law's house. I was hormonal and sobbing, and I was sure it was over. I stumbled out of the car and knocked on the door and she let me in.

"Is everything okay?" she said.

"I'm just *so angry* at him," I said. "I don't think he loves me. He doesn't touch me. He doesn't look at me. He doesn't initiate sex."

Carole cleared her throat but didn't say a word.

"It isn't how I thought it would be," I said. "Carole, I think it's over."

For the first time in her life, Carole took my hand. She led me over to the table and made me sit down. She gave me a glass of water and sat down next to me. "Jaime," she said. "Marriage is hard. My son is difficult. We both know that. He is not . . . affectionate. But I know for a fact that he loves you. And . . ." She looked down at her hands. "And so do I."

I stared at her. Was I hallucinating? Was she dying and finally had to say it to my face?

"You do?" I said, wanting to extend the moment.

"I do," she said, looking at me. I could tell she meant it. "Now please, go home to your husband. And don't take my grandchildren away. Please don't take them away."

And I realized I couldn't.

"Can I hug you?" I said, sniffling.

"Oh . . . all right," she said. It wasn't the longest, warmest, deepest hug I'd ever experienced, but it might have been the most significant.

I felt better. I felt more complete. And I realized that despite my imaginings and fantasies about raising my kids in Jersey, this was our home.

"Your son is just lucky he has a big dick," I muttered under my breath.

"Jaime!" she protested.

"Hopefully for you, it's genetic."

And from the living room, where my father-in-law, Papa Dave, was reading the paper, I heard him mumble, "It is."

"David Sullivan!" my mother-in-law exclaimed. I gave my father-in-law a high-five on my way out and went home, feeling much better. Was I becoming their people, or were they becoming mine? Maybe it was a little bit of both.

My own mother is no southern belle. From her, I learned to be happy in the moment. To be passionate and excited and loud and boisterous and to grab life by the balls and really live it up. But my mother is always temporarily happy. When everything is great, she is ecstatic, but when it isn't, she wears all her emotions all over her face.

From my mother-in-law, I've learned how to stretch happiness over the long term. How to see the big picture and appreciate delayed gratification. Whereas my mother waits for situations to make her happy, my mother-in-law defaults to happiness, and then deals with situations that come up. That's a big difference, and I've learned a lot about how to live in a joyful state from her. And when things aren't going well, my mother-in-law knows how not to let it take over her life. She would never let anybody see that she was at the end of her rope. It would be unseemly. My mother-in-law is now the person I go to when I am sad or down or confused or scared. She really is the quintessential southern belle. She maintains joy and poise through any situation.

It's strange and beautiful to live within the vortex of the opposition of my mothers. I've come to love it.

I like to think I've had an effect on my mother-in-law as well. Through me, I think my southern family has all learned to loosen up a bit, and even go a little off-color at times. Now Carole can utter a curse word or two without any real fear of bursting into flames. She's become a wonderful grandmother and she's become closer to her son than she ever was before I came along with the full-frontal hugs and demonstrative emotions I inherited from my own mother.

She also taught me about southern manners. (In fact, she gave me an etiquette book as a wedding present. Someday, I might actually read it.) Whenever I had a fight or disagreement with anyone in Birmingham, she was the one to call me and say things like, "Don't bother with them," or "Why do you have to be so aggressive? Why do you have to address everything head-on? There are better ways to do this." She was the one who said, "You don't have to speak to them, but you also don't have to be ugly about it." She was the one who told me, "Just be polite and smile and keep it moving." And she was the one to ask, "Why can't you just let it go?"

My answer was inevitably something like, "Because I'm not a Disney princess. This is how I live my life!" But the truth was, I was learning another way.

Sometimes our greatest teachers first appear to be our biggest roadblocks. I thought I was getting the short end of the stick, and I couldn't have been more wrong. Carole was everything I never knew I needed. Where I first saw weakness, I now see so much strength. When you open your eyes to what makes someone unique, you gain so much. Before I met Carole, I was moving at the speed of light. I was moving too fast to ever see what she had to offer. Too fast to really see her. She taught me to slow down and, if I don't have time to smell the roses, at least to notice they are there. My mother-in-law is a steel magnolia—not because she is cold and hard, but because she is a rare and gorgeous flower that cannot be crushed.

And I guess that's what a southern belle is: beauty covering a surprising strength. My friends remind me to write thank-you notes, to get gifts monogrammed, to show up at social occasions in the right dress and with the appropriate offering. Sometimes they teach by example—when I did a favor for Danielle around Christmastime, she came by and tied a big red bow on my mailbox. Adrienne always lets me know when I've committed a social faux pas, without ever embarrassing me. And Scarlett tells me how awesome I am whenever I need to hear it most. But these aren't the things that make them true southern belles. Love is.

Love beneath the etiquette, love beneath the traditions. Love of God, love of children, love of the other women going through the same journey. I can definitely relate to that.

Here are some things I've learned about southern women through my experience:

- They hold tight to their values. Whether I agree with them or not, I respect a strongly held belief more than the opinion of someone who agrees with me but could easily be swayed by the next smooth talker.
- They know who they are, but will sometimes change the surface view to match their men. I have a friend who was a staunch Republican and an Alabama fan, but when she got married, she became a strident Democrat and an Auburn fan. This seems to contradict holding on to values, but I think her true values never really changed—and among those values are: Stand by your man.
- They value marriage. They can be nasty about divorce, but keeping families together through thick and thin is the job of women in the South, and they do it very well.
- They always bring a hostess gift. "Oh, this white bean spread in this fancy jar with the ribbon? I just whipped this up today coincidentally, and thought I'd bring you some." Uh-huh.
- They will never let you know how much effort it takes and how much trouble they endure in order to appear effortless and untroubled.

- They can drink any northern man under the table. I've never seen any group of women who can drink like southern women. They can drink from morning until midnight and remain dignified, looking great, and holding cohesive and coherent conversations. I really don't understand how they do it. Nobody gets sloppy, nobody becomes violent. If I drank like a southern woman, I would be slurring my words and starting fistfights.

- They are ambitious for marriage and status rather than for independence and power, but through marriage and status they gain independence and power.

- They have secrets, and you are privileged if you get to hear them. Northern women tell one another everything without thinking much about it. In the South it is important to maintain an exterior that everybody's perfect and everything is fine. That's the story and they're sticking to it.

- Southern women are really very nice . . . until they're not. They are masters at talking out the sides of their mouths, like ventriloquists. Somehow, they think that means the insults don't count.

- In the South, "bless her heart" actually means "fuck that bitch."

- They like pimiento cheese sandwiches but they don't like, or even understand, lasagna, and they will be offended if you bring it to a party. Trust me on this.

- They dress their small children like it's the 1950s. Sailor suits and smocked dresses and all.

- They take the culture of kindness very seriously. They believe in doing unto others. They believe in helping others. They believe in courtesy and they will inconvenience themselves simply to help a friend.
- They withhold judgment, at least out loud.
- But if you break the southern etiquette code, you will be punished, one way or another. Your punishment will be civil but thorough.
- Southern women know that in the South, God is everywhere. They believe it, they live it, they promote it, and they aren't ashamed of it. And that's my favorite thing about southern women.

#cawfeetawk
The struggle is worth it.

Chapter 29

WHERE ARE THEY NOW?

*Y*ou know that thing they do at the end of movies, where they tell you how all the characters ended up? Well, you know how the South is. Things don't change very quickly. Leigh Anne is dating and has a job she loves. Scarlett still catches me when I fall, and Danielle is working on becoming a yoga instructor. Once, when I met Adrienne at the gym, I took one look at her and said, "You're pregnant."

"No I'm not," she said, turning red.

"Yes you are, you're pregnant."

"How did you know?" she said. "I haven't told anybody!"

A few months later, when she walked into a restaurant to meet me, I said, "It's a boy. Don't even bother with the ultrasound."

"Stop ruining all my big moments!" she cried. Of course I was right, and now Adrienne has one-upped me. She is the mother of three beautiful daughters and a son, and she is still in my life and with me every step of the way. Sometimes God sends people into your life because they are exactly who you will need when times get tough. So thank you, God, for Leigh Anne, and Scarlett, and Danielle, and Adrienne.

Perhaps the most significant lesson I've learned living in the Deep South is that you do not have to engage every battle that comes banging on your door. I spent my whole life fighting—starting fights, finishing fights, getting in the middle of other people's fights. I was in a constant state of war because I thought that as long as I was fighting, it would keep other people at bay and they couldn't hurt me. My mother-in-law taught me that being the one to smile first rather than the one who doesn't smile back is actually a better strategy in the long run. It may not be as immediately gratifying as a shot to the gut, but it's almost always more effective.

Carole and I are closer than I ever imagined we could become. She is always there for me, and although she doesn't withhold judgment when I misbehave—and although I probably won't assimilate as fully as she would like me to—we both love each other, and say so often. Carole sees how I love Michael, and the way I love Michael shattered every preconceived notion Carole had about me. She had never seen anybody love Michael like I did; though Carole doesn't always like my way, she loves the way I love her son. Deep down, although she prayed for it, I don't think she believed he would ever find a love like this. She didn't believe he would ever be a father. She didn't think he would ever get to come home to a woman who would love him forever, who would build a life with him. And now that I'm a mother, I understand how much that means, because that's what I want for my children, too.

And what about my children? What are they becoming?

Olivia is truly her own person, and southern through and through. She is eight years old, and has foiled and then exceeded every single one of my expectations. She has taught me more about boundaries than anybody else in my life, and her very southern admiration has helped me love the South more than anything else ever could. She recognizes our differences and is the first to say, "My mom talks to everybody. I don't do that." But she understands that differences don't matter. What matters is that we get up every day and try to communicate.

Max is seven, and I've grown to depend on him. Of all my children, he gives love most unconditionally. He looks at me, dazzled, and says things like, "You look beautiful, Mommy," and for just a moment I can see myself through his eyes. He is goofy and energetic and outgoing, and he loves attention. If anyone is ever going to teach him to be a southern gentleman, it will be Michael, but it's going to be a rough road, buddy, because Max has a good dose of Jersey in him. He's a little wild, but he's also full of love and hugs and cuddles, until he's ready to get up and run again.

Charlie is five, and in the looks department a dead ringer for her father, with that sandy hair and those same piercing blue eyes. But personality? She is more like me than either of my other children. Charlie doesn't care what anybody thinks about her. She will dress herself in outfits that don't match. And she's fearless. She marches to the beat of her own drum. She has the most infectious giggle, and it comes from the depths of her stomach. She lets it out as loudly as she can and doesn't care who's listening. Olivia has always been more aware of her surroundings, more in tune with who might be watching, but Charlie barrels through life like a bull. I'm afraid she's going to be that kid who is still changing out of her bathing suit at the public pool when she's seventeen because she just doesn't realize or care that anybody is paying attention.

She is the most Jersey of my kids. She has the thickest skin. And she might not turn out to be a very good southern belle—she might be the one who learns the rules but doesn't play by them—but she is a force of nature. I recently started recording and posting videos of Charlie when we say good night at the end of each day. I ask her questions and she's happy to answer for the world, bestowing her innocent and feisty wisdom. Through those videos, Charlie has brought more joy to more people's lives than I ever could have imagined or wished for.

And as for Michael and me? We take it week by week. I work daily on being the wife I want to be. I choose to forgive when I want to punish. I communicate when I want to shut down. I pray for him. I thank God for him. And he shows up every day doing the best he can. I watched Michael love me when I was unlovable and tried to push him away. I don't know how many times Michael has said to me, "I know what you're doing. I'm not stupid. You're trying to push me away, but I'm not going to go, so you can treat me like shit if you want to, if that makes you feel good, but it won't work. I'm not going anywhere." And that would just gut me, every time. The old Jaime would give in to worry and insecurities, and treat love badly until love would leave. That didn't work on Michael. He isn't going anywhere. He is mine, and I am his, till death do us part.

We may not be happy all the time, and I may not ever be the kind of person who can pretend I'm happy when I'm not (or stay quiet about it), but we are bound together forever. God saw to that.

#cawfeetawk

Not everyone is meant to grow with you. It's part of life. Don't spend too much time looking back at the past. You're not going in that direction.

Chapter 30

REAL WOMEN ARE
A WORK IN PROGRESS

A couple of years ago, I had an idea: My beautiful southern belles and I would make a great reality show. We had been through a lot together—bonding and breakups, births and divorces and deaths—but mostly we were becoming friends in a way I never knew was possible because of our cultural differences. And we were funny—our whole situation was funny. A New Jersey girl trying to survive in the Deep South? Who wouldn't want to watch that?

I pitched my idea, and the result was the Bravo TV show *Jersey Belle*. When the show was in its third week, fan emails began pouring in. It was amazing and heartwarming how women from all over, as far as Australia, were reaching out to connect.

Anytime you are your true self, for anyone to see, it can be terrifying, but viewers seemed to really appreciate what we were trying to do. In message after message, women wrote to me with words of encouragement. They loved the contrast between North and South, Jersey and Alabama, and they loved to see women coming together and supporting one another instead of tearing one another down.

People began asking my advice about life, love, and living in general (me? really?). I wasn't sure why they thought I had the answers, but I wanted to take the time to individually respond to every message. Soon, however, this became impractical. There were too many letters and too many questions. One morning, I decided to make a video. I grabbed my coffee, turned on my iPhone's camera, and said, "Good morning and welcome to cawfeetawk!" I was kind of joking with the name, but it was fun to say. I said something like, "Hey, you guys are writing me all these incredible letters, and I'm so glad you love the show! This is so new for me, and it's new for you, but I'm glad we're here together and I want to answer some of your questions."

That first day, eight people watched. I was amazed. I had *eight actual fans*! Soon that video reached over a thousand views and people began to leave comments, saying they loved seeing me outside the show. So the next morning, I did it again. "Hey, it's me again! Good morning and welcome to cawfeetawk!" And they responded again—"Do it again tomorrow, we love you, this is so much fun!"

At first I was just getting to know people, but a few shows in, I remember that I began commenting on a specific letter. I said something along the lines of, "Somebody wrote me about something she is going through, and girl, let me tell you this . . ." And that's when it really exploded. People loved it, and they began asking my advice on everything.

I didn't exactly give advice, though. Because what the hell do I know? We're all in this together. I was interested in just sharing our common experience, telling people how I handled something similar and how it worked or didn't work for me. I never told them what to do. I just wanted to share. I wanted to be friends with all of them, like we were all sitting down together, having coffee and talking about our lives. I looked straight into the camera and just talked like I was talking to a friend, and this was new for me because it made me vulnerable like never before. But I figured, hey, what the hell, I'm getting good at this vulnerability shit!

And as the audience grew exponentially, I began to realize that I am now in a position to help people who are in a place I used to be. Every morning, Michael still brings me a cup of coffee while I'm in bed, but now I share that coffee with anyone who wants to join me, and we talk. I mean, we *tawk*.

People come up to me all the time and they say I've helped them, but I can't even express how much *I* have learned from Cawfeetawk and the Cawfeetawk planet. I've learned more about life and love and self-esteem and family and parenting and insecurity and sex, and I've had to flip through my entire inventory of human experience to pull out anything that can help those who ask: my body dysmorphia, my miscarriage, terrible sexual experiences, being victimized, bullied, gossiped about, what it feels like to be mad at God, to not believe in God, to find God. *All of it.*

I know what it feels like to move to a new city and feel like you will never make friends, and I know what it feels like to make friends and not be sure they really are your friends, and I know what it feels like to lose a friendship after twenty-five years, and to say I'm sorry but I can't do this anymore. And I know what it feels like to finally let it all out and share it with others and listen to their stories, too.

Most of all, I've learned that right here, right now, I am exactly where I am supposed to be.

So, here I am. Like a twelve-stepper, grabbing the talking stick: "My name is Jaime and I live in Alabama."

It's been a long hard road, but I am still here. I've hatched many plots over the last few years—plots to move the whole family up to New Jersey, plots to whisk the children away and be free, plots to find Michael a job or at least find an apartment for myself where I could escape when life gets to be too much.

But then, I always think better of it. Alabama is my family's home. It is where we belong. My husband's family is here, and, frankly, my mother-in-law would probably miss me. And it is beautiful. And it is full of good people. And I have learned to love it.

So after nearly ten years, I am waving the white flag. Everything I've experienced has made me into the person I am today, and I believe God puts you exactly where you need to be. Although it is still sometimes hard for me to believe, Alabama must be where I need to be.

And my work is here. And my friends—my beautiful southern belles—are here. In this place, I continue to work at creating meaning for my life: motherhood, human connection, social responsibility, kindness. I don't know if I would have found this sense of purpose if I had been anywhere else. If I look at it that way, how could I not be happy that I'm here?

Most of all, this is where love is. I gorge myself on it. I'm drunk with it. I revel in it. And I'm saved by it.

Love has helped me to see so clearly what I couldn't see for so long, living down here below the Mason-Dixon line. Love

proves that despite all our differences, petty and profound—
despite everything we want for ourselves or think others should
want for themselves, despite our judgments and criticisms, our
mistakes and human failings, our tendency to look askance at
the "other" or favor those who are more like us, despite everything different between any two people—love wins. Love can
conquer prejudice, misunderstanding, human failing. Love can
conquer hate and violence and division.

We are all born into this world, and it isn't always easy,
and we don't always understand why we are here or what we
are doing, but God knows. He knows exactly what we need,
the lessons we need to learn and the moves we need to make.
Lessons learned, God. Thank you, with all of my heart.

ACKNOWLEDGMENTS

First and foremost, I want to thank God for choosing me. My salvation is my greatest gift.

Thank you to my mother for truly doing the best she could. I know how hard the job is and I didn't make it any easier.

My father for being the first person to love me for exactly who I was and letting me know that was possible.

Meredith, Carolyn, and David: my siblings, my lifelines, my accomplices, my allies. The Kardashians ain't got nothing on us.

Carole, a true Steel Magnolia; thank you for taking a chance on what scared you the most.

My Belles: thank you for stepping outside your comfort zone and befriending "that" girl. You are so beautiful and brave.

To the #cawfeetawk planet: I love you today and every day.

Thank you to Simon, David, and Eve for believing my story was worth telling and giving me the opportunity to share it.

Michael: thank you for walking this life beside me, and at times encouraging me to walk ahead. I love you.

Olivia, Max, and Charlie: I love you to the moon and back. You are my true pride and joy. *Good Night Gracie XO*

ABOUT THE AUTHORS

Jaime Primak Sullivan found fame as the star of Bravo TV's *Jersey Belle* and parlayed that exposure into a successful daily digital video series, #cawfeetawk. Jaime will soon star in the Facebook original comedy series *The Southern Education of a Jersey Girl*, produced by Trium Entertainment and Kin Community. Additionally, Jaime is the producer and host of *The Daily Perk*, a digital current events roundup that serves up the hottest headlines in pop culture and world news.

A career woman and a mom, Jaime and her husband are raising three children currently under the age of nine. Somehow, Jaime manages to run all aspects of her various businesses while juggling life as a busy mother, an adoring wife, and a (sometimes) reluctantly transplanted southern belle.

Eve Adamson is a nine-time *New York Times* bestselling author and award-winning freelance writer who has written or cowritten more than sixty-five books.